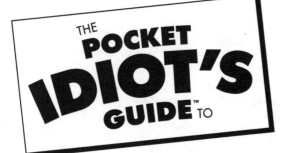

THE
POCKET
IDIOT'S
GUIDE TO

Surviving College

by Nathan Brown

ALPHA

A member of Penguin Group (USA) Inc.

This book is dedicated to the memory of my brother, Justin Thomas Brown (1975–1998). Rest in peace, big brother ... may you ride upon chromed horses in paradise until I can join you there once again.

International Standard Book Number: 1-59257-212-X
Library of Congress Catalog Card Number: 2004100488

06 05 04   8 7 6 5 4 3 2 1

Interpretation of the printing code: The rightmost number of the first series of numbers is the year of the book's printing; the rightmost number of the second series of numbers is the number of the book's printing. For example, a printing code of 04-1 shows that the first printing occurred in 2004.

Printed in the United States of America

Contents

Introduction

Leaving home for a university career can be a very scary time for anyone. For some of us, this is going to be the first time that we have ever lived away from our parents. For a few of us, this might even be the first time we have ever left the borders of our hometown. As is normal during any of life's experiences, especially new experiences, you are probably going through some unusual feelings— a little bit of fear and anxiety, mixed together confusingly with a good dose of excitement and enthusiasm. It is very much an emotional whirl-wind of joy and tears, making the transition from the life you have grown accustomed to into the beginning of a life you must learn to lead on your own. These are the years that will shape just who and what you will be in adulthood.

Don't feel ashamed that you are experiencing these powerful emotions, however. You are not alone, by any means. We all go through something like this sooner or later. Whether you are leaving home for college or simply leaving home for a life of your own, departing from the nest (so to speak) is an unavoidable part of life. No one can live at home forever (although I have met a few people who wish that they could). So ... when you finally spread your wings, are you going to fly? Or are you going to fall like a rock? If you are planning to fly, it might be helpful for you to know how.

How to Use This Book

This book gives you the basic knowledge and methodology that you will need in order to make the start of your college career a successful one. The first few weeks of university life (heck, the first couple of years) can seem quite overwhelming, especially with all the hustle and bustle of getting yourself situated. With this book, I have done my best to provide you with the means for making your transition into higher education as smooth as possible.

Extras

Throughout these chapters, you will notice that a number of different sidebars have been provided. These sidebars contain important information, facts, terms, and tips, as well as the experiences and the words of wisdom of real-life university students from colleges all over the United States.

Here are some examples of the sidebars that you will be seeing often as you read. Inside of each, you will find a brief description of what each of them refers to. Whenever you see one of these boxes, you may want to take note. The information in these boxes should be the most useful to you.

Campus Cautions

It's always a good idea to know where to find trouble. This makes it a lot easier to stay out of it. So in these sidebars I have provided you with warnings that will help you decide what to do—as well as what not to do.

It Could Happen to You

These are perhaps the most valuable little boxes of input in this entire book. While writing this book, I sent questionnaires to college students all over the country. I asked students to volunteer their personal stories about their experiences while in college. To those who were kind enough to offer up a piece of their lives, I would like to thank all of you from the bottom of my heart for making such an important part of this book possible. In order to protect the wishes and/or the privacy of certain individuals, their names, school names, and classifications have been withheld. In some sidebars, the names have been changed or last names omitted per the providers' requests.

Word, Yo!

In these boxes, you will find key terms, slang, and other college lingo along with their definitions. You will encounter lots of new terms in college, many of which are exclusive to the university world. Learn these terms so that you won't be confused when you first hear them.

Survival of the Cheapest

Money is a major part of higher education—mainly because if you don't have it, you can't afford to pay your tuition. Colleges don't come cheap, and every year things seem to get more and more expensive. In these sidebars you will find shortcuts, discounts, and other money-saving tips. With these, you may be able to ease the financial burden somewhat and give your pocketbook a reprieve, if a small one.

Acknowledgments

I would first like to thank the One Creator and the inexorable laws of the kosmos for allowing me to live this life while doing what I love as an occupation. I also thank my mother, for bringing me into this world and for always being supportive of me no matter what I am doing; my stepfather Bill, for always bragging about me at work; my little brother Jonathan, for fixing my computer and being my source at UNT; the entire Niday/Brown/Austin clan; Midwestern State University; University of North Texas; University of Houston; Half.com© and Ebay©; FastWeb.com©; all the students who were kind enough to contribute their knowledge to this book; my wonderful friends at Graham Central Station in Wichita Falls (for dancing, drinking, and laughing with me when I needed to blow off some steam); Kimberly Goe, for believing in me no matter what moronic things I do; Dr. Evans Lansing Smith, for showing me the way through the labyrinth; and Dr. Jeff Campbell, for being a devoted professor and one of my greatest mentors in understanding the world. I would also like to very much thank the editorial and production team at Alpha: Randy Ladenheim-Gil (Acquisitions Editor), Lori Cates Hand (Development Editor), Megan Douglass (Production Editor), Ross Patty (copy editor), and the rest of the staff who had a hand in making this book come to life.

Trademarks

Close Your Eyes, Hold Your Nose, and Dive Right In!

In This Chapter

- Navigating freshman orientation and class registration
- Getting started
- Being prepared
- Getting help from experienced students
- Smart textbook shopping

So you have decided to go to college? Woo hoo! Freedom, sweet freedom! Parties! No parents telling you what to do! Hallelujah, what joy! What joy! Okay, it's time to come back to reality, if only for a moment. The truth is, college can be a whole lot of fun (like a barrel of monkeys, only there aren't *really* any monkeys). However, if you don't start off on the right foot, you will find that things can get extremely un-fun, and very, very quickly. Don't worry. You won't let that happen, will you?

In this chapter, I discuss what you should expect during those first couple of weeks of university life—registration, orientation, the first day of class, and so on. I'll throw out some possible worst-case scenarios as well as some helpful tips so that you might avoid becoming one of those wayward freshmen who's wandering around campus, looking lost and pathetic, with that "deer in headlights" look in your eyes. Trust me, you will see this every single year, without fail, right around Fall orientation time—some new freshman, with a campus map in hand that he or she does not even know how to read, looking in every direction as if his or her destination will just suddenly reveal itself through providence in a ray of light shining down from the heavens to the tune of *Ode to Joy*. Yeah … unfortunately for them, that never actually happens.

After you've registered and gotten oriented, you'll need to buy your books. This chapter gives some hints on how to do that without having to take out *another* loan.

Plug into the Matrix: Class Registration

Registration for classes usually coincides with, and is scheduled into, the freshman orientation process. This (among many other things) makes attending orientation a must for any first-year university student.

Your Ticket to Admission

Before registration, of course, you must have already met the requirements for admission and have received a letter of admission. The requirements for admission into any given undergraduate degree program usually consist of the following:

- High school diploma or GED.
- Completion of SAT, ACT, or other state-approved, college-level admission exam with a satisfactory score as stated by the institution.
- High school transcript must meet the institution's minimum grade-point average requirements.

Most community colleges and trade/vocational schools do not enforce these requirements. Universities, however, do. So be sure you have met the these criteria and are an accepted student before showing up for registration.

Please Advise Me

It's quite common for first-year students to be required to consult with an advisor before they are allowed to register for classes. Do not feel insulted by this. No one is saying that you are not intelligent enough to choose your own classes. The advisor is there to make sure that you not only take the classes that you need, but also to stop you from taking on more hours than you can handle.

Advisors are often professors who are assigned to students based on their majors and minors (see Chapter 6 for more on choosing a major). For example, if you are a humanities major, then your advisor will most likely be a humanities professor. If you are a business major, you might have an economics professor advising you. Starting to sense a pattern here? I hoped you would.

But what if you are undecided, and are going into college as a freshman with an undeclared major? In this case, your advisor will most likely be from any random area of expertise. Remember that, just because your advisor is of a particular area of study does not mean that you must choose that area as your major. An advisor can often be useful in helping you to select a major, however. For even more information on choosing a major see Chapter 6.

Now Go Register ... Fast!

Once you and your advisor have worked out a degree plan and semester class schedule, you will need to go register as soon as possible. It is very important that you register right away because with every passing moment classes are being filled up and you might find that one or several of the classes you have scheduled are no longer open. This will send you right back to your advisor, which means you are back at square one. If you get to the registrar's office only to find a line that seems miles long, don't despair—you probably have other options.

Depending on your particular university, you might get lucky and be spared from the mind-numbing waiting and riotous chaos of class registration. Some universities integrate freshman registration into the orientation process.

Word, Yo!

Registrar—the name given to the person who directs the office that handles class registration and, at times, admissions for the student population.

Most universities are now equipped with both phone and Internet registration options, which you can usually access with your student PIN. You will probably need to get this number from your advisor. If your advisor can't give it to you, he or she can at least tell you where to get it. If you choose one of these options for class registration, you can find instructions on using them in either the undergraduate bulletin or semester class schedule. However, in most cases instructions are provided by either the automated system over the phone or on the website for online registration.

> **Word, Yo!**
>
> Undergraduate bulletin—a booklet printed at the beginning of each year by the university, containing instructions and guidelines for students as well as all new and existing campus policies. The Undergraduate bulletin also provides an organized list of class titles, along with a description of each.

Orientation or Disorientation? The Choice Is Yours!

When it comes to your freshman orientation, here is college survival tip #1: You need to, have to, and should want to go. I know it seems a little bit stupid. But trust these words—you will not regret having gone. Freshman orientation is there to help you. The university is not just doing it to give you something boring to do for no good reason. So please, do yourself a favor and listen to your parents for once—*go!*

Orientation Perks

While you are at orientation, you will receive some of the essentials needed for living, studying, and even surviving on campus. For example, you will receive your student ID card, which you *absolutely must have* in order to do even the simplest of things on campus such as check out a library book, buy a textbook in the Campus Bookstore, use the computer lab, and even just eat in the cafeteria. On some campuses, you might not be able to get into your dorm unless you have it (so try not to leave it in your room). Without your student ID, you could wind up bookless, helpless, hopeless, homeless, computer illiterate, and hungry. That doesn't sound like fun to me!

Word, Yo!

Orientation—In colleges and universities, an event for first-year students that provides them with a chance to orient themselves with the most basic aspects of university and scholastic living. Most often, universities *require* beginning freshmen to attend orientation.

Meet the Upperclassmen

Orientation is also a perfect opportunity for you to get acquainted with some of your university's senior classmen (something that will come in handy to you later). These students have been in college for a while—most definitely longer than you have, in any case. Senior classmen know what's going on, even if you don't, and it never hurts to have at least one who is able to recognize you by name. A senior classman who refers to you as "that freshman" or "the new guy/that new chick" does not qualify as someone who recognizes you "by name."

Campus Cautions _____

Rule #1: Do not, under any circumstances, allow yourself to lose your student identification card. Keep it in the same place you keep your driver's license, or go out and buy one of those groovy key-chain necklaces and wear it around your neck, or get a new body piercing and hang it from that if you must—just *do not lose it!*

Rule #2: Find out in advance how to get a replacement student ID, just in case you screw up royally and find that you have already broken Rule #1.

Freshman orientation is most often run in large part by students who have already completed their freshman year. Find one of them, stick close to them, and pay attention. Don't be shy with upperclassmen. They were once freshmen just like you, and they know what it feels like to have questions—so don't be afraid to ask them. Besides, you might be the one who asks the question that everyone else has been dying to know the answer to but was too afraid to ask. Listen for what senior classmen say when someone else asks them a question (before you interrupt them later with what will be considered a now-stupid question because it has already been answered).

It Could Happen to You

A buddy of mine skipped his orientation because some jerk sophomore told him that he didn't need to go (some people like to play jokes like this on freshmen) and that orientation was nothing more than a tour of campus. Taking this guy at his word, he didn't go. The first day of classes, he was a mess—didn't have a student ID so he couldn't get into any of his labs. One class' room and time was changed, but since he wasn't at orientation to find out, he missed the entire first class trying to find it and learned that it started two hours ago. *Don't* believe what anybody tells you—go to orientation!

Jonathan Brown—Senior, University of North Texas

Be Prepared

Okay, so you have gone to freshman orientation. Good for you. Orientation is just the beginning of all things new and chaotic. However, whatever you do to prepare yourself for the start of classes once orientation is finally over is totally up to you. That's right! No one is going to tell you what to do from this point. But don't panic! Let's begin to prepare for the battles that lie ahead.

Try to think about possible worst-case scenarios before they actually happen to you (but try not to dwell on them or you will start having that dream about being naked in the hallway at school again). Then come up with possible methods for preventing them from catching you off guard. For example, if I know that I have no clue where my classes are, then I might need to go find them.

Make a "Dry Run"

It will behoove you to make a "dry run," so to speak, *before* the first day of classes has actually started. This will prevent you from being late to class on the first day. To tell you the truth, being late on the first day is not that big of a deal. However, it never hurts to make a lasting first impression on your professors by starting out the semester with a little polite punctuality. Try to think of it in the same way you would think of brushing your teeth—no one is going to raise a big fuss about it if you don't, but everyone is going to notice.

Try to make a game out of this: Get your schedule, pack a lunch (or not), grab your backpack, and take a walk. Find your classes, one-by-one, in the order you would go to them if class were actually in session. Know the names of the buildings your classes are in as well as the classroom numbers.

Memorize the last name of every professor you have. Why? Well, if the room has been moved come game day, you can then ask someone, "Where can I find professor so-and-so's class?" instead of "Where can I find my English class? It's supposed to be in room B200 but there's no one in there." This will almost always be immediately followed by another question—"Who is your professor?" Not knowing the answer to this not only makes you feel really stupid, it creates more work for the person you are asking. Nobody likes having to work more because of someone else's ignorance. By the way, if your schedule has listed the word "Staff" under the professor's name for one of your courses, please don't be one of those students who actually thinks this is the prof's *name*. "Staff" simply means that a professor was not concretely chosen to instruct the course before the schedules were printed up. So no ... there is no one named "Dr. Staff."

Another thing you can do, if you have the backbone, is to locate the offices of each of your professors while on your dry run. If they are in, take a brief moment to introduce yourself to them and perhaps inquire about what you will and/or will not need for the first day of class. Never miss an opportunity to get inside information—especially when it's coming straight from the horse's mouth. Remember that professors are only human beings, just like you and me. There's no reason to fear them (yet).

Campus Cautions

Never, ever refer to one of your professors as a "teacher." They really hate it when students make that little screw up. A professor has had to go to a heck of a lot more school than an ordinary "teacher" has. "Dr. so-and-so" (for a Ph.D.) or "Professor so-and-so" (if he or she is not a Ph.D.) are appropriate methods for addressing them. If you are unsure as to whether an instructor has a Ph.D., just use "Professor so-and-so" until either they correct you or you find out they are "Doctor so-and-so."

What (and What Not) to Buy for Class

Speaking of that first day of class, let's discuss what you are going to need (notice I said "need," not "want"). Do not go out and buy all of your textbooks beforehand (unless you took my advice and have already spoken with the professor), because you might not need some of them. Also, the listing of required books might have changed—it has been known to happen—and, if it does, you might as well kiss the idea of selling back your book goodbye. The campus store rarely buys back books that are no longer listed by a professor (of course, they have no problem selling them to you).

Here is a list of some universal essentials that are a must-have for any student:

- One three-ring binder per class (at least). You will need this to keep your notes separate and organized for each class.
- One package of college-ruled notebook paper or a spiral-bound notebook (for writing out notes).
- Pens
- Pencils (you can never have too many pencils)
- One packet of Scantrons (these are why you need plenty of pencils)

 Word, Yo!

Scantron—a form used for administering multiple-choice exams that has become standard for most colleges across the United States. You must use a No. 2 pencil. Scantrons enable a computer to quickly grade hundreds of exams in a short amount of time.

- One or more "blue books" per class (these are used for writing class essays; some schools provide them for students, so check first)
- Scientific calculator (for math and science courses; the professor may specify a brand/type, so you might want to wait on this one)

- Two 3-inch floppy disks
- Day-runner/day planner/calendar
- One pocket folder (specifically for syllabus/syllabi and other handouts)

A Little "Brown-Nosing" Never Hurts

On your first day of class, if you have not done so already, it would not hurt to approach your professor and introduce yourself. Heck, you could even ham it up a bit and ask him/her a question or two, as long as they are related to the class.

This will put a warm fuzzy in your professors' hearts and big star on your forehead in their eyes. Remember that first impressions are very important. Most professors have well over a hundred students, and first impressions are often what they base their opinions of you on for the rest of the time you are in their classes.

Mention Any Scheduling Conflicts

Last thing, professors hate surprises. If you have any religious holidays/holy days that are going to coincide with his class (such as Ramadan, Hanukkah, and so on), the first day would be the best time to mention this and hand him or her a list of them. It's vital to make sure the professor is aware of them as far in advance as possible. The last thing you want to do is be a burden to the one in charge of your final grade.

Get with Some More Experienced Students Than Yourself

You are suddenly a very little fish swimming around in a very big pond. Your best chance at survival? Find some bigger fish and make friends with them. If you are into philosophy, think Thomas Hobbes. If not, think of those little dinosaurs that ganged up on and ate that guy in *Jurassic Park III*.

Your best avenue of approach for meeting older students is to become involved in student organizations (at least one). The presidents of clubs and student groups are almost always very friendly and helpful. And if you are a likely candidate for joining their organization, they will tell you just about anything you want to know. Usually, there will be a time during your orientation when you will be given a chance to acquaint yourself with the different student organizations available and the leaders of student government (see Chapter 4 for more on student organizations).

Smart Textbook Shopping

Textbooks can be a real pain in the pocketbook for any college student—you can't afford 'em, and you can't live without 'em. It is a classic college-style catch-22 of epic proportions: The universities make a load of money by selling used textbooks to you, while you get the short end of the stick when trying to sell them back at the end of each semester. They give a student $10 for a textbook that they will turn around and sell to another student for $50. So how can you keep this from happening? Or at least, how can you lessen the monetary burden of textbook buying and selling? Read on!

eBay Your Way to a Cheaper Textbook

What a great time to be a college student! Unlike our parents, we have been blessed with the almighty World Wide Web. Online textbook shopping is great because it cuts out the middleman. Instead of buying used or new books for a small fortune and then selling them back to the campus bookstore for a fraction of what they're going to turn around and sell it to the next naïve student for, you can sell it online for your a profit. Selling and buying your books online means you can sell your texts for less than any campus bookstore can, adding $10 or $20 to what you get in return. On the flip side of things, you can find almost any college textbook online and have it shipped to you within a few days, which means you spend less money on your textbooks.

So where do you find a place online to buy and sell textbooks? I'm glad that you asked. While there are plenty of options available to you with only a little bit of web surfing, the easiest and least expensive way to buy your textbooks online is through a site called Half.com at www.Half.com. Half.com is a spin-off of the popular eBay auction site, and a very lucrative way to buy and sell used and rare books. What is so appealing about Half.com is that, instead of having to list your books on an auction for a limited amount of time, you can list your items indefinitely and for a set price. No guessing, no hoping, and no getting charged a fee whenever your auction expires (because there is no auction). Half.com is also a great place to locate used text-books. So if the campus bookstore has no more used copies of a textbook you need, you might want to check out this site before you buy a brand new one.

Campus Cautions

When shopping for textbooks online, you will need to be sure that you read the item descriptions very carefully. A book that is listed with the cheapest price may be that way for a good reason. It might be missing several pages, it could be missing the cover, or it may be riddled with a bunch of underlining and illegible notes. Unless these things do not really matter to you, you will want to know as much about the condition of the textbook that you are buying as possible. Half.com requires that all sellers provide full disclosure about the product. Sellers who do not comply with this policy can have their selling privileges revoked.

The New Edition Trap

Another downside to reselling your textbooks at the campus bookstore is that sometimes professors

decide to switch to an updated version of a textbook, or to a different textbook altogether, for the
next semester. This means that your book is now
worth next to nothing to the campus bookstore.
Once again, the Internet comes to the rescue.
Chances are that someone, somewhere, is still
using the textbook at a different university. One
person's trash is another's treasure, as they say. Post
your books online and it will improve your odds of
selling an outdated textbook.

The Least You Need to Know

- You need to go to your freshman orientation, whether you want to or not.

- Be prepared! Have your basic supplies on
  hand and do a preliminary dry run before
  classes begin.

- Get to know other students—especially
  those who have been involved in university
  life for a while.

- Buying and selling textbooks online can save
  you big bucks.

My Mom's Not Here? Somebody Help Me!

In This Chapter

- Doing your own laundry
- Feeding yourself
- Cleaning up after yourself
- Getting out of bed
- Keeping from getting sick

Whether you like it or not, there will come a time when you will have to realize that your mother did not come to college with you. The upside to this is that she is not there to make you clean your room or to pick up your clothes, wash dishes, wake you up, or any of the other countless things she's done for you all your life. The downside is, she is not there to make you clean your room or to pick up your clothes, wash dishes, or any of the other countless things she's done for you all your life.

So before you find yourself wading through a knee-deep pile of dirty clothes, sniffing around for a shirt that's not too stinky to wear, you need to learn to do your laundry. Before you find some strange fungus living in your bathroom, you need to clean it. Before you flunk out of school for missing class or for excessive lateness, you better learn to get your rear out of bed on time.

In this chapter, I cover some basic housekeeping skills and a little domestic how-to, so that you don't end up smelly, sick, and/or lonely (nobody likes the smelly kid in class). It's a lot like jumping out of a burning airplane during a nosedive in the sense that you do not have to like it, but you *do* have to do it.

Keeping Up with the Laundry Piles

If you have never done your own laundry before, you will need to pay special attention to this section. In fact, just take this book with you the first time you decide to do laundry (which should be in the first weeks of school) … just in case you forget something. This could save you from an extra trip for quarters and/or a wardrobe-ruining mistake.

A Thing Called the Laundromat

Most likely, you will have to use a Laundromat, maybe for the first time. If so, be sure to bring plenty of quarters with you. There is nothing worse than getting to the Laundromat only to find that the change machine is either broken or empty.

Also, be sure you know how much a load costs before you drag your laundry down to the Laundromat. You do not want to wash your clothes and discover that you don't have enough money to *dry* them (wet clothes are really heavy, too). Usually, washing a load of laundry will cost you about a dollar—but the price varies from one place to the next. In some places, it can be as little as 50 cents; in others, it could cost you as much as $1.50 per load. Don't forget that you are going to need to dry those clothes, too. So don't forget to factor in the dryer costs which, ironically, are usually higher than the cost of a washer. Why? Because they know you won't leave once you have a load of soaked clothes. On average, a dryer will cost from 75 cents to $2 depending on location and how many times you have to run your load through to get it dry.

The best method for estimating the total cost of your trip to the Laundromat is to separate your laundry into loads (a little less than an armful) and count out enough quarters to wash each load once and dry it twice. So if the machines cost a dollar to wash and $1.25 to dry, that will be $3.50 per load. If I have three loads, I know that I am going to need at least $11.50. You might not use all of that before you're done. However, Laundromats are notorious for having shoddy or malfunctioning dryers.

How Not to Ruin Your Clothes

Once you've got your clothes, your quarters, your detergent, your fabric softener, and enough time, head on down to the Laundromat. But do not get ahead of me. First of all, you cannot just throw all your clothes into a machine, dump in some soap, and voilá! Laundry, unfortunately, does not work that way.

First, and very important, you need to separate your clothes into three types: light colors, darks/blacks, and whites. Then you need to weed out any clothes that require special attention, such as delicates, loose-knit sweaters, or spandex. Check the label on the tag if you have any doubt about this. Some clothes are not machine-wash friendly (maybe they require hand-washing or dry-cleaning instead) and can be ruined that way.

Always be certain to check the labels on your clothing, evenly distribute each load in the machine (not too much on either side), and properly measure your detergent. Remember that scene in *Mr. Mom* where Michael Keaton has to duke it out *Rocky*-style with an out-of-control washing machine? Too much detergent or an unbalanced load and you might find yourself doing the same thing.

Try to pay attention to what the last person who used a machine was washing and doing. If they were bleaching a load of white linen, you do not want to use that machine to do your darks. Residual bleach can hang around in a machine for a few cycles and it might bleach your darks and/or colors. Some people use public machines to dye their clothes. Like the bleach, someone who was dying their canvas bag black might inadvertently dye your white satin sheets as well if you use the machine after they do. Always look into a machine before you go tossing your clothes into it.

 It Could Happen to You

I once put a load of colors into a Laundromat machine, among which was a brand new $50 shirt. Apparently, whoever had used the machine before me had been bleaching their linen. My clothes came out of there looking like a bowl of Lucky Charms. Everything had faded into everything else. My new shirt? Ruined, never worn, and I couldn't even return it to the store.

J.V.B.—Senior, University of North Texas

After you have separated your clothes into different loads, you need to treat each as follows:

- **Whites**—This includes white sheets, men's and women's white underwear, white T-shirts, and white socks. Whites should be washed on the Warm/Hot or Hot setting. Be sure not to accidentally leave a dark or colored article of clothing in this load.

Otherwise, you might end up with an entire load of pink underwear (anything red will do this), or your white sheets may be gray when you pull them out (black socks can do this). You might want to add bleach to a load that is exclusively white. If so, remember to add bleach *only after* the washer is agitated (this means the little spiral thingy in the middle of the water has started mixing up the clothes and all the clothes are saturated).

- **Colors**—This includes towels, colored sheets, light-colored jeans and socks, and t-shirts (not white). You should wash these on the Cold/Warm or Warm setting. Some types of detergents contain a color-safe bleach; if you opt to use this kind of detergent, you may want to read the label before using it on certain kinds of clothes.

- **Darks**—Darks include black socks, dark-colored jeans, slacks, jackets, and just about anything else that's darker than a worn pair of blue jeans. You should wash darks on the Cold setting in order to avoid bleeding and fading.

- **Delicates**—These are articles that require particular attention. These include women's undergarments and blouses, and certain types of sheets and towels (such as those made of satin). Some machines and dryers have a Delicate setting. If not, cold is always a safe bet. Remember, however, to always read the labels on your clothes before attempting to machine wash them. Materials and washing instructions vary from one article to the next.

For trouble spots or stains, there are numerous spot/stain removers available on the market. The campus mercantile store often carries these. "Spray & Wash" is great for this and very easy to use.

Hung Out to Dry

As far as drying your clothes is concerned, be certain that you place clothes in the dryer only if the label on each article says that it can be machine dried (you cannot machine dry pantyhose). Otherwise, an article that cannot be machine dried must be hung out to dry (shower rods are excellent for this). Remember that if you have a new article of clothing that already fits you snugly, you might not want to machine it—otherwise, it might shrink and become too small to wear.

Campus Cautions _____

Public Laundromat machine dryers are often *very hot!* Keep an eye out and be careful not to burn your clothes by over-drying them.

One Cannot Live on Pizza Alone!

I know, we all love to eat pizza, sushi, and Chinese takeout. They're tasty, convenient, and (the best part) you do not have to cook them. However, a steady diet of fast food is not only a little unhealthy, but it can also get very costly. Eventually, you are going to have three choices:

1. Break down and go eat in the cafeteria with your student meal card (hey, if you get hungry enough, it will happen).
2. Starve to death (I do not like this one).
3. Learn to cook or make something that you like (preferably something edible).

Always try to eat at least twice a day. Low blood sugar can affect brain functions, give you a sour mood, weaken your immune system, and cause chronic fatigue. It is understandable if you do not like the types of food offered in the campus cafeteria, but it can't be worse than going hungry (can it?).

Quick and Easy Cooking

Most often, dorms have rules restricting the use of hotplates, and dorm rooms do not come with kitchens (at least none that I've ever seen). However, there are no rules against making peanut butter and jelly sandwiches. Sometimes a dormitory will have one communal kitchen area for the entire building. Unfortunately, this could mean waiting in

a long line if you want to use it during normal eating hours as everybody in the building tries to
nuke their food in the same hour using the same
microwave. However, most of the time you are
allowed to have a small, economical refrigerator in
your room. They can run you anywhere between
$50 to $150.

Campus Cautions

Due to concerns over fire safety, most
university dorms do not allow students to
have the following items in their rooms:
candles, hot plates, grills, microwave
ovens, incense, hookahs, bongs, or pipes.

If you happen to live in your own apartment or in
a dorm that allows them (and, these days, some
actually do), get yourself one of *George Foreman's
Lean, Mean Grilling Machines*. They are pretty
fire-hazard safe, a cinch to clean, and can grill a
sandwich in just a minute or two. You can make
everything from grilled cheese to chicken teriyaki
with one of these babies.

Eating on the Cheap

For cheap food options, remember that the following items can often be found for less than a buck:

- **Ramen noodles**—you can make this with
  a little water and the microwave in the

students' common area (usually they have one). You can sometimes find these for as cheap as six packets for a dollar.

- **Macaroni and cheese**—You can find the generic kind for as little as three boxes for a buck. Warning: too much of this can stain your teeth yellow.

- **Rice in a box**—comes in a variety of flavors (chicken, beef, broccoli and cheese, etc.) and it is dirt cheap—about a buck a box or less if you keep it generic, but remember that you've got to at least have milk to make it most times (usually you can get away without using the butter that the instructions ask for).

- **Spam**—with a little rice and seaweed, this makes a tasty treat called Musubi. Otherwise, create Spam concoctions at your own risk. I've heard that mixing Spam with mac and cheese will do terrible things to your sphincter. Apparently, it has something to do with a catalyst effect that hot grease has on powdered cheese.

This Is Not *Animal House* ... Clean Up After Yourself

Do yourself and your roommate a favor ... try not to turn your living area into a pigpen. This doesn't mean that you have to become an anal-retentive clean freak, but it does mean that you need to keep the clutter level as close to a minimum as possible. Besides, a floor covered with trash and dirty clothes can be unsafe and a fire hazard—not to mention smelly.

Reasons to at Least Make an Effort

Don't leave last night's pizza box sitting on the arm of the couch for a week. All kinds of nasty bugs and viruses can grow on old grease, and the last thing you want to do is catch one of them and make yourself sick.

A clean dorm room also provides you with a much better environment for studying. It also makes organization easier and helps you to avoid losing things (like a syllabus). Last but certainly not least, it allows you to get that oh-so-happy refund of your safety deposit just in time for summer break.

Don't forget that most university dorms have a Resident Advisor (RA), who (depending on how vigilant he or she is) might make random and frequent checks of the dorm rooms. You do not want the RA to walk in (he or she *will* have a key) and find your room looking like a tornado just blew through it. You can be disciplined or fined by the university for this ... or even asked to find somewhere else to live, especially if the problem continues after repeated warnings. Save yourself the headache of living on your RA's bad side and do your best to be, if not neat and tidy, then at least fairly sanitary and uncluttered.

Essential Cleaning Supplies

In case domestic chores and cleaning are totally foreign concepts to you, the following is a list of cleaning supplies that you might want to have handy so that you can keep your living area from becoming the "pig sty" that your mother always scolded you about:

- Vacuum—you might want to invest in a small hand-held vacuum instead of a full-size one (which you probably won't have room for anyway). In some dormitories, there is a community full-sized vacuum that you can sign out from your RA.

- Broom and dustpan

- Sponge mop or Swiffer

- Glass cleaner (old newspapers are a nice and cheap substitute for paper towels)

- General-purpose cleanser (I recommend some 409 or, for the very nasty cleanup, Grease Lightning)

- Air deodorizer (preferably the disinfecting kind)

- Dusting spray and rags (they also now have disposable wipes for this on the market)

- "No-scrub" foaming cleaner (use a couple of times a week to avoid mildew and soap scum, or buy an "after shower" spray and use after every shower)

- Large and small sponges

- Paper towels or disinfecting disposable wipes
- Dishwashing liquid (for hands and any dishes you might have; remember that washing each dish as you use it keeps the dishes from piling up in your sink or other sickening places)

If you plan on keeping food around, you might want to invest in some plastic storage containers for things like pasta and cereal. You might not have had bugs crawling around the kitchen back home, but if you are not careful you can definitely end up with them in your apartment or dorm room. A cockroach crawling on your face can be a nasty wake-up call.

No More "Five More Minutes, Mom" for You ... Wake Up!

Some mornings you will wake up and wish that your mother were here to drag your rear out of bed, whether you want her to or not. However, your mother does not fit into your suitcase and you cannot (and probably should not) bring her with you to college.

Consequently, your mother is also no longer around to tell you when to *go* to bed. There is nothing wrong with an occasional late-night cramming session, but on most nights you will need to get at least eight hours of continuous sleep. A regular sleeping schedule will make the all-night study groups a lot more tolerable when they do occur … and they will.

According to Dr. Frank Wichern, a psychologist with a practice in Dallas, Texas, the "last two hours" of an eight-hour sleep period "are the most important" because it is during this time that the brain has a chance to resolve worries, fears, and insecurities. Too much sleep deprivation can cause any human being too become paranoid, cranky, and a little bit weird. Four hours is not a good night's sleep; four hours is a nap. Don't walk around campus like a zombie because you decided to go to penny draft night at *Doogie's House of Hops.*

Campus Cautions

The last two hours of an eight-hour sleeping cycle are the most important for the body and the mind. This is when your mind deals with anxieties and concerns. So try to schedule things so that you can maintain a regular sleep pattern that includes at least 8 hours of sleep, if not 10.

A midday nap can be very healthy if you can do it without missing or being late for class. Taking a nap in the early afternoon can be especially beneficial if you are planning on having a late night.

Remember, however, that nothing is better than a good eight hours of sleep.

If you are the insomniac type, experts suggest that you adopt a regular sleep cycle. This means that you go to bed at the same time every night and wake up at the same time each morning. Doing this allows your brain to develop a habit of sleeping during a particular period. This not only makes falling asleep easier, but it makes waking up easier as well and lessens the occurrence of oversleeping.

The Importance of Being Hygienic

The importance of keeping clean, aside from keeping up an organized appearance, has mostly to do with avoiding illness. Regular showering/bathing, detailed dental care (brushing and flossing at least twice a day), and washing your hands, especially before and after using the restroom (even more so if it is a public restroom) are all essential to keeping your body as free of bad germs as possible. The fewer germs you are carrying around, the less likely you are to catch some nasty bug. A dormitory can turn into a nesting ground for all kinds of "campus crud." Some of this stuff can make you miss classes; some of it can be deadly.

Protecting Yourself

In a communal living environment, such as is found in college dorms, sicknesses spread like wildfire. All it takes is for one student who lives in the dorm to get sick. That student gives it to his/her roommate and/or boyfriend/girlfriend. They give it to others, and you can guess how it goes from there.

Your best line of defense against contracting the vast array of colds, viruses, or worse that are going around is good personal hygiene. Wash your hands frequently and keep a can of antibacterial spray such as Lysol in your room. Also wash your linens often, especially after you have been sick.

Remember that taking good care of yourself will do wonders to lessen your chances of getting sick. A healthy diet, getting enough sleep, and keeping your alcohol consumption in check are all essential for ensuring that you stay well and sick-day free. Tired, hungry, and hungover is not a pleasant way to spend a day, trust me.

Less Illness = Fewer Absences

Cleanliness might be next to godliness, but we are more concerned with your healthiness and its effect on your attendance. Sick days can cut into your classes. Remember, it takes only a few absences to get yourself dropped from a course. Even if you have understanding professors, you are still going to be playing catch-up on missed readings and assignments. It's never good to fall behind, not to mention that missed classes mean missed lectures … which, of course, means that now you have to track down someone who takes good notes. (And if you weren't actually at the lecture, you have no way of knowing whether someone else's notes are accurate.)

The Campus Killer: Bacterial Meningitis

A major concern on college campuses around the country is the spread of bacterial meningitis. Not only is bacterial meningitis extremely contagious, but it can also be *fatal* if it's not caught and treated in time. To prevent the contraction and campus-wide infection of this illness, many campuses are offering meningitis vaccinations.

It Could Happen to You

I had mono in the last semester of what was supposed to be my senior year. I was so sick that I couldn't get out of bed for two weeks. Obviously, I missed all of my classes. Most of my professors were willing to let me catch things up. But in one of my core classes, I missed a major exam and several quizzes. The professor was the hard-nose type and refused to let me make up anything. I got dropped with an "F" and was unable to graduate. Now I'm here for another whole semester just to make up one piddly little course.

Anonymous—School and classification withheld

Some universities are now even offering those vaccinations free of charge. If your university is one of these, be sure to take advantage of it. Even if it's not free, it would be in your best interest to shell out a little money to get this shot. It's much better than the alternative, I have to tell you. Just talk to someone who has contracted this disease. It makes mononucleosis (also called "mono" or "the kissing disease") look like a walk in the park on a fall afternoon.

The Least You Need to Know

- Take enough quarters to the Laundromat; separate your whites, colors, and darks; and read the labels to keep from ruining your favorite things.

- Try to supplement your fast-food diet with a few trips to the cafeteria or some cheap and easy meals you can make yourself.

- Save your health and keep your roommate and RA happy by making an effort to clean and straighten your room or apartment.

- To get up and get to class on time (as well as feel rested and alert), get eight hours of sleep every night.

- Good hygiene, taking care of yourself, and vaccinations will help you avoid getting sick.

Chapter 3

Dear Mom, Please Send Money

In This Chapter

- Managing your finances
- Making the most of a little money
- Working through college
- Taking advantage of student discounts
- Loans, grants, and scholarships

Money cannot buy love or happiness, but it can make them a lot easier to find. The truth is that without money you cannot live. Up until now, most of you have not had to worry too much about money—that was Mom and Dad's job. So unless you are lucky enough to have unlimited credit at the "International Bank of Mom/Dad," you will need to know how to manage your own financial affairs.

In this chapter, we discuss some of the basics of financial survival—how to balance a checkbook, create a budget, and more. We will also discuss credit card (a.k.a. "The Plastic Devil") do's and don'ts, how to avoid credit pitfalls and tricks, and how not to end up having to quit school just to pay off your debts (which happens to college students all the time). Lastly, we deal with scholarships, loans, and grants to help ease the burden of tuition costs. So before you call the number on the back of that "pre-approved" credit card with "a low starting interest rate," be sure to read through this chapter.

Balancing on the Checkbook High Wire

My advice to you—*do not* get a checking account unless you are ready and willing to keep decent track of one. If you are not, it will only cost you more money and could become a dangerous temptation that you can certainly live without. Don't become one of those students who ends up playing Russian Roulette with payday, writing checks that migth or might not clear before the money to cover them actually gets into your account. The best way to avoid this problem is to simply not allow yourself access to checks. Besides, modern technology offers you the miracle of the Automated Teller Machine (ATM) card, which you can use to access your savings account. With an ATM card, you have access to only the money that is currently in your account. There is no risk of bouncing checks or overdrawing your account balance.

A Safety Net

Are you ready for the responsibility of a checking account? Better yet, is it a responsibility that you would welcome? If so, then you may forego my previous warning about not getting a checking account, pass go, and collect $200 (not really, this isn't *Monopoly*).

If you decide to get a checking account, you should make sure it includes some form of *overdraft protection*. Basically, overdraft protection means that if you ever write a check that exceeds what is in your checking account, the bank will take money from elsewhere and deposit it into your checking account in order to compensate—instead of just allowing the check to bounce, which is going to cost you even more money in penalty fees. Some banks do this by using two separate accounts, usually checking and savings. If you overdraw on a check, the difference is taken out of your savings account and transferred over to checking. Other banks do this by providing customers with a credit cushion. When an account is overdrawn, the money is credited to the customer until the discrepancy is resolved. You do have to pay back the money, however, and sometimes with interest.

Finding the Right Balance

Once you have a checking account, it is crucial that you balance it regularly. These days, many banks provide customers with a 24-hour telephone or Internet access service to checking accounts, which customers can use to find out which checks have recently cleared and what their current account balance is. Despite this, you should do your best to keep track of your transactions with your checkbook. Banks make mistakes, just like everybody else, and you don't want to lose money because of someone else's screw-up.

Word, Yo!

Overdraft protection—a failsafe provided by some banks for customers with checking accounts. If a customer writes a check that exceeds their account balance, money is taken from either another account (such as savings) or a bank-funded credit line in order to compensate for the difference.

Here is a rough example of how to balance a checkbook. The appearance of the checkbook ledger may vary from one bank to the next, but the basic idea remains the same. Basically, you record your transactions and then calculate your new balance after each one.

Transaction Description	Deductions	Deposits	Balance
Paycheck		$800.00	$800.00
Electric Bill	$85.00		$715.00

Transaction Description	Deductions	Deposits	Balance
Dinner at Restaurant	$20.00		$695.00
Oil Change and Tire Alignment	$156.00		$539.00

You should go over your checkbook at least once a day on days that you have used it. Doing this will keep things from piling up on you. Do not procrastinate until you are so far behind on your transactions that it turns the simple task of balancing your checkbook into an impossible burden that haunts you in your sleep. Financial worries can cause some hardcore insomnia.

Campus Cautions

When you file your taxes each year (the deadline is April 15, if you didn't already know), be sure to include the student tax forms that the university business office should send to you (or your parents, if they plan to claim you on their tax return as a dependent). These will ensure that you (or your parents) get the proper tax deductions.

Living on a Budget

Even if you don't have a checking account to balance, it's always a good idea to keep some kind of an organized budget plan. Keeping yourself on a budget prevents you from overspending or sending too much money to the wrong place. Trust me, it's not fun to realize that the money you spent the night before on dinner, drinking, and dancing has caused you to be $50 short on this month's rent.

An Example Monthly Budget

If you have never kept a budget before, here is an example that might help:

Monthly Budget: September

Deductions and Deposits	Amount	Balance
Income	+1,000	$1,000
Class expenses	−100	$900
Tuition payment	−200	$700
Rent	−200	$500
Food	−150	$350
Entertainment	−100	$250
Miscellaneous cushion + emergencies	−100	$150
Surplus total		$150
Savings = ½	−75	$75
Remaining		$75

It's best to overestimate your deductions and to underestimate on income. Whatever remains after you have made your initial calculations will be your *surplus total.* Divide your surplus total in half and, whatever the amount, put it into a savings account (and *leave it there*). Hopefully, you will have a little left after this. This is your *remainder.* Remaining money is there for emergencies in those last few days before payday—not for you to add to your entertainment expenses fund.

Luxuries and Other Expenses

Whatever amounts you have allowed for luxury expenses, such as entertainment and food, should be followed to the penny. This might require a little extra planning on your part. For example, know how many times you can afford to eat out for that budget period and stick to it (no compulsive eating out or splurging unnecessarily). Try to spend a portion of your food fund on some *actual* grocery items (see Chapter 2).

If you have a car, don't forget to deduct for insurance payments (please have at the least liability insurance) and gas money. If you have any medications that you have to take regularly, make sure that you deduct for them. At least once a month (for the love of Pete), you will need to check on your hygiene items. If you find that you do not have enough of something to last you through the rest of the month, add the cost of that to your deductions under "Hygiene expenses."

If you plan on calling home a lot, I'd suggest setting aside some money for phone cards each month. Trust me, you do not want to use your room line to make long-distance calls. Those phone bills have a tendency to sneak up on you. Stick to phone cards ... they are already paid for and you can't use them more than you can afford them.

 It Could Happen to You

One Christmas shopping season was all it took to nearly end my college career. I got a few pre-approved cards in the mail and used them to buy gifts for all my friends and family. My parents thought I'd either won the lottery or was dealing drugs when they saw this. After I told them about the credit cards, I think they'd rather wished that I *was* a drug dealer. I had to quit school for an entire semester just to pay them off—$5,000 plus interest. One interest rate shot up to 29.5 percent after I'd had it only 6 months.

Anonymous—Senior, University of North Texas

When the Money Runs Out, You Gotta Get a Job!

It's a sad but true fact—if you make too many mistakes with your money, it *will* put an end to your college career (or at least postpone it for a while). Don't let this happen to you. Don't let material possessions and immediate gratification threaten your future. The best way to avoid a life of low-wage servitude without education? Get a part-time job!

Work-Study Jobs

Many campuses now offer work-study programs where students can work and live on campus while taking classes. They offer many different jobs, from janitorial to secretarial. Whether mopping floors, making copies, or doing data entry, these jobs are perfect for a student who needs some extra cash for living and/or tuition costs.

Campus bookstores are also a good place to seek seasonal employment opportunities. They often hire extra helping hands during the fall and spring rush periods.

Townie Jobs

If work-study is not for you, no problem. College towns are full of all kinds of seasonal and part-time job opportunities. Since a large part of a college town's population lives there for only nine months out of the year for four years at a time, many of the local businesses have an extremely high turnover rate on their employees. The best time to look for employment in a college town is either just prior to the beginning of a semester or right before the end of one.

Remember that tipping is not a city in China! A waiting, busing, or bartending job that pays minimum wage plus tips can be very rewarding, especially those in restaurants and bars that are frequented by large numbers of students and profs (professors are good tippers most of the time).

Of course, if the job is not within walking distance of campus, you will need to have a car or make sure that the job is accessible by public transportation.

Avoiding the Credit Card Trap

A credit card can either be your best friend or your worst enemy. Keep in mind that a credit card is not there to act as a license for you to live beyond your means. It is there, however, to provide you with spending power when you *need* it. For example, if your tire blows out on the freeway and you have to be at work in only a few hours, the credit card is there so that you can pay for the repairs and get to work on time. You get the new tires, you get to keep your job, and everybody's happy.

However, a credit card is not a method for you to pay for that $1,500 entertainment center you have been ogling at the electronics store, or that $1,200 dress that you have been drooling over at the mall. If you keep your credit card exclusively for "need-only" items, you should not have any problems that you cannot handle. However, let yourself go on a single frivolous spending spree at the local mall and it can turn around and bite you in the you-know-what before you can scream "bankruptcy."

It Could Happen to You

Minimum payments? What a joke! I kept paying and paying. It took me six months to realize that my balance was going down, oh, let's see ... only two dollars at a time! I called the customer service number to tell them they had made a mistake. The operator explained that the minimum payment covered interest, monthly service fees, and a few dollars of the balance. I felt like an idiot. Minimum payments? What kind of a sick person came up with that whole scam?

Anonymous—class and school name withheld

The Evil Minimum Monthly Payment

Credit card companies just love to get their hooks into college students. Why? Because we really love to spend money but do not have very much of it, which means that we would really enjoy having a credit card, but can only afford to pay the minimum amount required of us each month.

You know what that low minimum monthly payment means? It means your balance will not go *up*, but it will also never go *down*. Sure, the "low monthly payments" make a credit card sound affordable. But what credit card companies often fail to mention is that this payment covers little more than the interest that they tack onto the owed amount every month.

Paying the minimum $50 or so payment does little to impact your actual balance and, in some cases, your balance might actually go up. This happens when some sneaky little credit scam company puts an interest rate on your card so high that it exceeds your minimum monthly payment. That way, you keep dishing out the cash and they keep dishing out the interest and the debt. And, if you are not planning on paying *at least* twice the minimum payment each month, it could take you the rest of your natural life to get a card paid off.

The Right Way to Build Your Credit

A good way to build up some nice points on your credit report is to get *one* card and go to the store. Buy some items that you can afford (meaning you have enough *cash* to pay for them), but pay for them with your card. After the purchase, go home and write out a check for what you just bought and immediately mail it off to the credit card company. Do this once a month. Do not use the card for anything else and *do not* get another card. This method will rack up a nice credit history for you that will come in handy when you find that you *need* more credit.

Stretch Your Buck to the Limit

Who says rich people have all the fun? Whoever said that does not know the power of a dollar.

Heck, for a dollar you and your buddies can go to the dollar store, buy a pack of cheap balloons, fill them up with tap water, and make a trip to the nearest bridge overlooking a jogging trail (though I take no responsibility for what might happen to you if you accidentally pelt a 250-pound muscle man with an airborne water balloon). The point is that there are plenty of fun things to do for little or no money. All you need is a little imagination.

For a $5 cover charge you can drink penny drafts 'til 10 o'clock. Every college town has a bar with a "penny-draft" night. If not, they've got something close to it. Keep your eyes and ears open for good deals on a night out. Ask around. You will eventually find somebody who will know where to find cheap drinks, no-cover clubs, and so on.

Remember, your tuition or activity fee is paying for more than just classes, room, and board. That money also goes toward on-campus entertainment, such as sporting events, plays, movies in the auditorium, free on-campus concerts, and more. However, you will need your student ID to attend these events free. Don't let that money go to waste … take advantage of these free events.

Remember that

- Parks are free.
- Walks are free.
- A cup of coffee rarely costs more than $1.50.
- Conversations don't cost a thing.

- Frat parties rarely charge a cover.
- A good time is not measured by how much it costs.

Survival of the Cheapest

Remember that student ID? Well, aside from giving you access to library books and the campus cafeteria, it can also be your ticket to free stuff and money savers. Many businesses that surround a college campus offer discounts to anyone with a student ID.

Loans, Scholarships, and Grants ... Oh, My!

Unless you were born into a rich family or plan to pay every cent of your tuition costs out of your own pocket, you are going to need a loan, a scholarship, or a grant. But how? Why? And where in the world do you find these things? Where do you find money for college? Well, I found out for you.

First of all, you need to make sure that you have secured a reliable method of payment before classes even start. When deciding between a loan, grant, or scholarship, it will be important for you to know the difference between these three. A loan from the state or federal government, bank, or private lender will require that you repay the money (with interest) within a set period of time. A scholarship (the best option, in my opinion) is awarded to applicants based on certain criteria. This money is given, free and clear, as long as you maintain any requirements set out by the scholarship such as grade-point average minimums or simply writing and mailing a thank-you note to the donor who funds it. It does not have to be paid back. Grants are usually given without need for repayment as well, although the requirements are a bit more strict and they often require a lot more paperwork.

 Survival of the Cheapest

Military reservists receive money for college under the Montgomery GI Bill. They don't have to pay back this money.

Student Loans

Applying for a federal student loan can be very beneficial, if you ever manage to finish the terribly large pile of paperwork that it entails. I have known students who have had to suffer through as long as a year and a half of paperwork trying to get a federal loan approved. The good thing about federal student loans, however, is that you often have a very long time to pay them back, and rarely do you have to make payments until after you have graduated college. Federal loans that do have

interest have much lower interest rates than any
loan received from a private lender.

Student loans offered by banks are sometimes a
better option than a federal loan. The payment
requirements are often nearly identical, although
the bank will most likely add some interest and will
not give you as long to pay it back. However, it is
faster than the federal loan route, and often banks
will work with a student's future plans to determine
the method and timeline of repayment.

Campus Cautions

A federal loan or grant (such as a Pell
Grant) can be a great way to pay for college. But receiving one is a very slow
process that involves a lot of paperwork.
But if you have no other options, you'll just
have to tough it out.

Scholarships and Grants

Scholarships and grants are probably any student's
best bet. They do not take as long and have a lot
less paperwork than a federal loan, and there are
plenty of them to be had. However, getting a
scholarship/grant requires that you be somewhat
ambitious because it will be up to you to track
them down and acquire them. Remember, a scholarship will require you to meet certain criteria

throughout the school year, whereas a grant will most often not. No one just gets handed a scholarship out of the blue (do they?). You have to work for it.

First, you will have to find a scholarship or grant that you qualify for. Often, scholarships/grants are given to a particular type of student—some are specific to the applicant's major, some to the applicant's athletic skills, and some to the applicant's parents (such as children of veterans). Still others are offered based on a student's situation, such as scholarships from the United Negro College Fund and those offered only to homosexual students.

One of the best online resources for locating college scholarships and grants is a site known as FastWeb (www.fastweb.com). At FastWeb, you can fill out a profile questionnaire that, when completed, will be run through a giant database of available scholarships and grants. Those scholarships and grants that have requirement criteria matching your particular profile will be collected and sent to your account with basic information and a link to the scholarship's website. An initial profile application can produce hundreds of potential scholarships. Membership to FastWeb is free, and it's fairly easy to use.

Once you have located a fitting scholarship, you will need to apply for said scholarship. Most scholarship applications require that you write an essay on a given subject. Ham it up as much as possible on your application and try to put some effort into your essay. Write anything and everything on your application (as long as it is *true*) that you have ever done which might make you appear better than the next applicant—awards, honors, accomplishments, charity work, military service, athletic achievements, and extra-curricular activities are all good things to have on your scholarship application. Understand that you are attempting to convince these people that you are not only a worthy student, but a good person who deserves to be given their money.

The Least You Need to Know

- Keep track of your checkbook. Don't let it get behind and pay for a mistake later.
- Keep an organized budget plan. Don't jeopardize your future by overspending.
- Don't get duped by credit card companies. Have a card for emergencies and do not live beyond your means.
- If you are running out of money, it is time for you to get a job! A little tough labor never killed anyone.
- There are lots of ways to have fun in college without spending a lot of money.
- Low-interest loans, scholarships, and grants are out there to be had as long as you are willing to hunt them down and apply for them.

Chapter

Get a Life! Join a Group and Meet Some People

In This Chapter

- Greek life—sororities and fraternities
- Student organizations
- Other ways to meet people and make friends on campus

There are student groups for every stroke of every folk! No matter how antisocial or out-of-place you may think you are, there is an on-campus group where you will fit right in! For example, fraternities are no longer just beer-guzzling boys' clubs—there are frats for scholastic honor societies, religious fraternities, and ethnic-specific fraternities. If you cannot see yourself getting involved with the whole Greek scene, there are still a variety of social, scholastic, and special-interest student groups for you to choose from.

In this chapter, I talk about the various types of student organizations that are available on college campuses, as well as other ways to meet people and fit in. Remember that every university is different, however, and you will need to carefully check your particular university's policies regarding student groups before doing anything mentioned in this chapter. Without the availability of student groups, university life could become very lonely for many of us. So take a look at this chapter, and perhaps, you will be able to find the place that is right for your interests and passions.

Living the Greek Life

These days, the university Greek world has come a long way. So before you start letting visions of *Animal House* and *Revenge of the Nerds* dance in your head, let's take a toned-down look at the reality of today's fraternal orders and sister sororities—both social and honorary. Unless you are looking to do some time in jail, by the way, panty raids are not a good idea.

Greek Speak

The following is a list of definitions to aid you in familiarizing yourself with some Greek terminology.

- **Fraternity**—"Frat" for short. According to Webster's Dictionary, "a brotherhood, actual or in a formal association, as a college *fraternity*." Normally, fraternal organizations are exclusively male. However, in recent years certain types of fraternities have begun to allow females to pledge.

It Could Happen to You

I pledged to join a sorority as a freshman, but after pledging and getting in, I only stayed in for 6 months. I just did not have the time to participate in any of it. If you're going to pledge Greek, make sure you have a schedule that allows for it.

Jana King—Senior, University of North Texas

- **Greeks**—In colleges and universities, an umbrella term commonly used to describe members of a university fraternity or sorority, due to the use of the Greek alphabet in naming each particular group. Usually, this term applies to social fraternities/sororities and is rarely used for members of scholastic groups.

- **"Hell Week"**—A slang term used to describe the week when newly recruited pledges are initiated into their brotherhoods/sisterhoods through some type of ceremony (very often a humiliating one, in the case of certain fraternities). However, many universities now forbid the open use of this term by fraternal organizations. Also, any hazing (physically, mentally, or emotionally abusive initiation rites) is strictly prohibited by all universities, usually by a no-tolerance policy. All participants in hazing can face disciplinary action (most likely expulsion).

Campus Cautions _____

Extreme forms of physical hazing are not only dangerous; they are forbidden and illegal. Remember that a prank can turn tragic at the drop of a hat. In the past, students have been maimed, scarred, and even killed by fraternity pranks and hazing practices. If you see or experience hazing, you are in the wrong place. Report these violations to the proper authorities at once (despite the intense peer pressure not to).

- **Pledge Week**—A week when campus fraternities and sororities hold campaigns to recruit new pledges for the upcoming semester.

- **Pledge**—A new candidate in a Greek society who has not yet completed the initiation ("Hell Week") process. A pledge is not yet considered a full member by their brothers/ sisters until a formal initiation has been completed.

- **Sorority**—In colleges and universities, a female-specific sisterhood that often exists (but *not always*) in association with a particular fraternity, as in a "sister sorority." According to Webster's dictionary, a sorority is defined as "a girls' or women's organization."

To Pledge or Not to Pledge

Although joining a Greek society can be a fun and beneficial experience, any student advisor will tell you that it is best to hold off on pledging to one until after your freshman year, or at least your first semester. Remember that freshman year is already going to be stressful enough as it is—especially if you are planning to take on a full load of class hours (which you probably shouldn't do, either). So if you plan on pledging, make sure you are well informed on what is going to be required of you. Don't go Greek until you are certain that it will not put a strain on your time or your grade-point average.

Campus Cautions

Being in a fraternity or sorority can end up costing you a lot more than just time. Pledge dues, formal wear, and special Greek events can get pretty costly. Make sure you know what a fraternity is going to cost you on average before you pledge and find that you can't afford it.

It Could Happen to You

I only knew one person on campus before I pledged with my fraternity, Phi Kappa Sigma. It was one of the best decisions I could have made. I had access to a lot of stuff that most freshman do not, like fraternity brothers who'd already had some of the same profs that I was taking and knew what *not* to do when writing papers and taking exams. Being in a frat also gave me a great group of guys to hang out with and a band of big brothers that I could look up to.

Jonathan Brown—Phi Kappa Sigma, University of North Texas

Honorary Fraternal Organizations

If you feel that the entire Greek world is a very chauvinistic and male-dominated system, then there are alternative fraternal orders you might wish to consider. Understand that many *honorary* fraternal organizations are no longer limited to male members. Most scholastic organizations, such as Mortar Board and Sigma Tau Delta (the International English Honor Society), as well as most humanitarian fraternities, for example, currently allow for a nongender-specific, coed pledge environment for new society members.

Word, Yo!

Honorary fraternity—A fraternal organization that usually invites members to join based on scholastic merit or volunteer/community service. Due to their nonexclusive policy toward gender (allowing both male and female members) as well as their often being referred to as "Honor Societies," these groups are referred to as "honorary" fraternities.

Finding Student Groups

There are plenty of other student groups to join if the Greek life is not your cup of tea. For example, English Club, Fencing Club, Spanish/German/French (plus other foreign languages) Clubs, and Theatre Club are just a few of the most commonly found student organizations on just about any university campus.

Join a club and you will also find other students who are in the know on the local nightlife, which means you will be able to probe their brains for every bit of helpful information that you can! Examples: Where do people hang out? Where do people *not* hang out? Where's trouble and how do you find it (or avoid it)? Is there really an Olympic-size swimming pool on the roof of the dorm (there is not)? Anything you are curious about can be answered by joining up with just one student organization.

Here are some examples of common student groups, arranged by their respective categories:

- **Scholastic/major-related groups**—English Club, Spanish/German/French Club, Math Club, Philosophy Club, College Bowl Team, Academic Decathlon, Internet Trivia Competition Group, Student Government Association, Theatre/Speech Club, marching band, and others.

- **Athletic groups**—*Special interest:* Fencing Club, Swimming/Diving Team, intramural sports teams, atomic Frisbee (a.k.a. Frisbee golf), Cricket (the game, not the bug) Club, Judo/Jujitsu Club. ***University teams:*** football, basketball, baseball, soccer, rugby, tennis, golf, lacrosse, and more depending on what activities are provided by your university.

- **Special-interest groups**—Society for Creative Anachronism (SCA), Gay-Straight Alliance, Parents and Friends of Lesbians and Gays (PFLAG), Pan-Hellenic Society, Black Students' Union, International Students Organization (ISO), Student Diversity, Chess Club, Caribbean Student Organization, and more.

If you consider yourself an activist for a particular cause/charity, or would like to become an activist for one not listed above, check out your university's student organization listing for a group that supports it. Remember, if you don't ask, no one is going to tell you.

Of course, it would take an extremely long time for us to list all of the university groups that currently exist in the university world, so if nothing here catches your eye, it doesn't mean that nothing will when you get to your school. Should none of the above interest you, be sure to investigate exactly what your college has to offer before you simply give up on ever finding one.

Okay, Forget the Clubs ... Let's Just Meet Some People!

Okay, the idea of joining a club has failed because you are either too lazy or too busy. It has now become necessary to do the unthinkable: Go out and meet people on your own.

The Common Area

Every college/university has a student common area, although some institutions refer to it as the student center, the student lounge, or the student union. This location is specifically designed for the purpose of general congregation, study groups, and all-around snack munching for the entire population of the student body. If you hang out in the student common area long enough, you cannot *help* meeting somebody new (although I refuse to accept any responsibility for what type of person this might wind up being).

It Could Happen to You

When I first got to college, I was from out of state and did not know a soul, on *or* off campus. So I started doing most of my class reading in the Student Center. After about a week, certain faces started to become familiar and it became a kind of an elite little club. I did not even realize this until one night I did not go. The next afternoon, I showed up and everyone asked me where I had been. I had not imagined that any of them noticed I was even there, let alone gave a damn if I left. I still kick myself for not speaking to one of them sooner. Turned out, we all had a lot of stuff in common.

Anonymous—Sophomore, Midwestern State University

Overcome Your Fears

The simple truth of the matter is that we are all scared to death when we first arrive at college (look around you and you will see that fear is in everyone else's eyes, too). We are all so out of our minds with the fear that we will not be accepted by other students, or that we will end up being alone and bored, that we never even try to prevent it. Well, guess what? This is not high school, and the "cool-kid"-dominated social hierarchy is a thing of the past. The social structure of a university is a black-and-white difference (and better) from the one you knew before—so you no longer need to be terrified of being socially excluded. No one is going to call you a nerd just because you always know the answer in class (in fact, people will flock to you in college because of this).

Getting involved with as many campus events as possible and opening up to other students is the very best thing that you can do to meet new and interesting people while making strong, lasting friendships. So go ahead and leave your fears at home … you won't need them anymore. *Carpe diem*! Let each of us seize the day and never allow such unnecessary fears of rejection and ridicule to prevent any of us from making our college experiences some of the very best years of our young adult lives.

The Least You Need to Know

- Joining a fraternity and/or sorority can be a very fun and rewarding experience. Just make sure that you know what you are getting yourself into.

- There is a wide variety of student groups on campus, so take some time to look around for the one that is right for you.

- With a little bit of courage and just a hint of confidence, the student center/common area can be the perfect place to meet people.

Chapter **5**

Dude! This Place Is Full of Freaks!

In This Chapter

- Being open-minded
- Tolerating other religions
- Understanding alternative sexual preferences
- Dealing with racial and ethnic diversity on campus
- Surviving the roommate from hell!

It won't be very long before you start to discover that there are certain types of individuals in your new environment who seem extremely odd and foreign to you (okay, maybe they're the freakiest things you've ever seen). No matter how well-rounded a person you think you are, up to this point in your life you have really been exposed to only those things that were allowed to you by your environment (and by your parents).

However, the shelter of your childhood has now been removed a bit and the blinders are off. Your eyes are open … so try not to look too surprised when (not *if*) you find yourself rubbing elbows with other students who do not share the exact same values, beliefs, backgrounds, or even the same sexual orientation as yourself. If you turn into "Mr./Mrs. Defensive" and/or become standoffish when you encounter students such as these, you will soon discover that your number of friends keeps decreasing while your number of enemies keeps increasing.

In this chapter, we deal with the religious, ethnic, and sexual diversity found on the common college campus. We will also cover some tips to help you deal with the new and unusual people you will meet (not to mention that weirdo they will probably give you as a roommate at the dorm).

Open-Mindedness Is the Key

So what, exactly, are you supposed to do about all of these strange and new individuals? Am I suggesting that you should just abandon your entire belief system and morality structure to become the hell-in-a-handbasket-bound heathen that your parents always warned you to stay away from? No, I am saying nothing of the sort. You will not be required to do anything quite that extreme. In fact, you can achieve tolerance of diversity by implementing only one simple tool: an open mind.

It will be most important for you to remember to keep a reasonably open mind when dealing with fellow students who are of different races, genders, religions, and sexual orientations than your own. Let this be your motto—"Live and let live."

No matter how mainstream you think you are, you will meet new people at college who disagree with your opinions. No matter how off the hook you think you are, you are going to meet new people who actually agree with you for once. There is no reason for anyone to feel like a freak because, let's face it, on some level we are all a bunch of freaks. That's what college is all about—experiencing the new and unusual. I'm a weirdo, you're a weirdo, here a weirdo, there a weirdo, everywhere a weirdo, weirdo. So it's all good.

Religious Tolerance

A key element to achieving religious tolerance is for you to understand that what has always seemed right and true for you may not have ever seemed right or even true for someone else. Does this mean that all your religious beliefs are wrong and worthless? Absolutely not. This simply means that you must realize that right and wrong is no longer an issue when it comes to dealing with students of different religions, and that everyone has the right to believe in any particular god, deity, or "higher power" they feel is correct (just as you do). There will even be those who do not believe in a God at all, and they, too, have that right. Have you ever heard the old saying, "Agree to disagree?" Well, that's kind of the same thing as this.

Believe in whatever you need or want to believe in while you are at college, but you cannot expect everyone else in the university (or the world) to simply abandon their own religious faiths and fall in line with yours just because theirs is making you uncomfortable. This is just not going to happen ... so get over it and get to class.

Word, Yo!

Tolerance—according to Webster's dictionary, it means "liberality towards the opinions of others; patience with others."

There is nothing wrong with being curious about other religions, especially ones that you have never encountered. Doing research at the library, asking questions, and attending diverse religious services are all good ways of learning to understand the religions around you.

Campus Cautions

Patriotism is one thing, but stupidity is another! Terrorist jokes are bad form in the presence of Muslims (and anyone else of Arabic descent). If you just have to make a bad, ridiculous "Osama Bin Laden's mama is so fat ..." joke, make sure you are doing it in the right company.

It Could Happen to You

Don't let anyone try to force his views on you, and don't try to force your views on him. You don't have to agree with, or even like, the other guy's opinion, but you do have to give his beliefs the respect you'd want him to give to yours.

Jason Bennett—Sophomore, Midwestern State University

Alternative Lifestyles

Nobody likes a vocal homophobe (aside from another vocal homophobe, perhaps). And you'll rarely see bigots invited to parties. Please do not become one of these people. As stated earlier, your exposure to the outside world has been limited by your environment and parents up 'til now. You will find that it's very easy to feel inclined to react negatively to that which is strange to you. It's okay to feel awkward, just don't let it affect you to the point of making you unable to get past it.

Practicing Tolerance

Yes, there is homosexuality in college (and the world). There *always* has been; always will be. Deal with it. Likewise, if you're militantly gay, don't try to make others feel guilty for being "breeders."

Campus Cautions

"Queer" and "fag" are terms that most educated people know well enough not to use. Using these terms could quite possibly (and most likely) label you forever as ignorant, a bigot, and/or a neo-Nazi, prejudiced redneck. Unless this is how you *want* to be perceived, just do yourself a favor and refrain from saying them.

As mentioned earlier in regard to religion, it is not necessary for you to practice, condone, or even accept sexual practices you disagree with. However, it is necessary for you to allow others to do as they wish without being judged, harassed, chastised, or threatened for their choice of lifestyle.

Alternative Lifestyles at a Glance

Here is an at-a-glance reference guide covering some of the different sexual orientations that you might encounter while at your university. Just remember: "to each his own (or her own)."

- **Heterosexuality**—Those who are sexually attracted to members of the opposite sex.
- **Homosexuality**—Gay males and lesbian females, both having a sexual orientation that is for same-sex relationships. Despite what you have heard or where you were

raised, "queer" and "fag" are inappropriate terms to use. So don't. "Gay" is a perfectly appropriate and safe umbrella term to use. Just stick to that one if necessary. A homophobic, or "homophobe," is someone who is afraid to the point of violence when in the presence of homosexuals. If you are one of these, do everyone a favor and stay away from the gay community, or at least just learn to keep your mouth shut. And remember, "gay-bashing" is not just an ignorant and bigoted act—it's a crime.

 It Could Happen to You

Once I went dancing at a bar I'd never been to. Apparently, some local guys at this place got the idea that I was a homosexual. Later that night, they followed me out to the parking lot and beat the $#!^ out of me. I got gay-bashed without the benefits! I'm *not* even gay! How ignorant is that?

Anonymous—Junior, Midwestern State University

- **Bisexuality**—Being sexually attracted to members of both the same and opposite sex. Despite this double-sided sexual orientation, bisexuals are more-often-than-not monogamous. So should you find yourself dating a bisexual, try not to allow your insecurities about their attraction to your opposite sex destroy your relationship.

- **Uni-sexuality**—Okie-dokie. Roughly, this is love of one's self. These people are attracted (sexually) to themselves. Yeah, I know ... I thought I'd heard everything, too.

- **"Open" relationships**—Okay ... treading lightly, now. These are people who have relationships that are nonmonogamous, bringing other people and couples into their beds. Also known (mainly during the '70s) as "swingers" or "wife-swappers," they are into swapping sexual partners with other couples, having sex parties, orgies ... you get the idea.

- **Transgender**—An umbrella term including anyone whose gender is not clearly defined as either male or female. Transvestites, hermaphrodites, transsexuals, and any other nongender-specific group fall into this category. While it can be difficult to address someone when you aren't sure of that person's gender, try not to make your confusion too obvious. Do not allow your confusion to cause you to behave cruelly toward such people. Understand that for most of them this life was not a matter of choice (any more than it was your choice to be born male or female). Hermaphrodites and transsexuals, nine times out of ten, were *born*, not *"made."* So if you have insecurities with this, try to stay out of the way. If you can't or won't, then just keep your mouth shut—live and let live!

Racial and Ethnic Diversity

While at college, you will be exposed to other students and human beings of every shape, size, creed, and color. This has the potential to be a wonderful learning experience for you, but only if you are brave enough to take advantage of it. With an open mind and a forgiving heart, you will be able to learn more about the rest of humanity than you ever imagined possible.

Everybody likes to meet a well-rounded person. Well, college is your chance to learn how to become that person. Seize it! Don't be one of those students who leaves high school to enter college and hang out with no one but the same kind of people they hung out with back home. Expand your world a little! That's why your parents are sending you to college in the first place (or, at least, it should be).

Do not look at diversity as a problem, but instead as an opportunity for you to grow as a student and as a human being. Smile at people! This makes it a lot harder for others to dislike you! Educate yourself by asking questions and (heaven forbid) make a trip to the library if you wish to know more about a new culture that you have encountered. You might discover that, in the end, none of us are all that different as human beings.

Be respectful of the cultures of others and remember—*live and let live!* Now go, young grasshopper, and achieve your enlightenment—and stop trying to snatch the pebble out of my hand ... it's annoying.

Campus Cautions

Do not refer to people from Asia as "Orientals." Most Asians consider "Oriental" to be a racist and offensive label (and a kind of rug). "Asian" is the proper term to use.

Despite all that you have just read, if you still truly desire to hang out only with those students who are of your own particular make and model, there will be more than enough opportunities for you to do that as well. Universities are crawling with numerous and diverse student organizations that are available to the student body for exactly this purpose (or vice versa). So if need be, you should take advantage of them. Heck, you should take advantage of student groups anyway. How else are you going to meet anyone besides your maniac of a roommate? Speaking of whom ...

Dealing With the Roommate from Hell!

Sad but true—you can pick your friends, you can pick your nose, and you can even pick your friend's nose (if that's your cup of tea), but you cannot choose your roommate in the dorm during your freshman year. This one is out of your hands. In the melting pot of communal living that is university life, there is a pretty good chance that you will clash with your roommate on one level or another. Living with someone is never easy—especially a stranger.

The truth is that, just because you have to live in the same room with a person, it doesn't mean that the two of you have to be the best of friends. In fact, there is no rule in the student handbook requiring you to even like your roommate. You don't have to hang out with him or her if you don't want to. And you definitely don't have to let that person make you feel miserable all the time. Welcome to what some like to call "real life," where you will have no choice but to learn to get along with other people, even though you do not necessarily like to be around them. Yes, your parents were right about this one.

It Could Happen to You _____

My freshman semester of college, I ended up with two roommates from Mexico. They could speak English just fine, but only did so if they were speaking to me directly. At first it made me feel really paranoid. Then I found an upside! Now I can curse and order alcohol in perfect Spanish!

Anonymous—Sophomore, Midwestern State University

Chill Out and Make the Best of It

First of all, try not to be a control freak about the room that you share. Remember that this is a living space for both of you, and neither of you has the right to dictate to the other. Your roommate's space is your roommate's space. Your space is your space. Easy enough? If your roommate lives like a pig, that's his own business and not your problem (unless his mess is invading your mess). When this happens, do your best to keep things civil and, most important, do not be anal retentive with the person you are living with … it's annoying.

Most universities tend to loosen the reins on dorm living once a student has completed his/her freshman year. So if anything, you can have the hope that, no matter how bad your roommate situation is during your first year of college, it's only temporary. So don't become one of those students who gets all weird, depressed, and downtrodden over how much you cannot stand your roommate. It's kind of pathetic.

Also, remember that there is no rule stating that you have to spend all of your out-of-class time in your dorm room. So if you don't like your roommate, stay out of your room as much as possible. Find somewhere else to study. Find another place to kill time. Do not add to the already high stress level of your freshman year by spending all of your time in the one place you do not want or need to be.

Last Resort: Call the RA

Okay, worst-case scenario—you've done as instructed and find that none of this is working. Time to call in the *resident advisor* (RA). This should be your last resort. If you cannot handle the conditions with your roommate, then it is the resident advisor's job to handle such situations. Often they can either help get you into a different room with a different roommate (who probably won't be any better than the one you have) or at least do something to help resolve any domestic disputes you two might have.

Word, Yo!

Resident advisor—referred to as an *RA* for short. Normally, an *RA* is a student (sophomore class or higher) who lives in the dorms and functions as a superintendent of sorts, helping new students get settled into their rooms, keeping the peace, and reporting building/room maintenance needs. Be nice to the RA ... they tend to be slightly edgy individuals and seemed stressed out all the time. You know, I wonder why that is?

The Least You Need to Know

- When you enter college, you will be exposed to all the many wonderful, interesting, eccentric, and just downright weird types of people that inhabit this planet.

- Try to keep an open mind and do your best to immerse yourself in all of the different races, genders, lifestyles, languages, and religions that you encounter while in college.

- Do what you have to in order to get along with, or at least tolerate, your roommate. Remember that he or she is probably just as frustrated with you as you are with him or her.

Chapter 6

Class?! You Mean They Were Serious About That?

In This Chapter

- Getting to class
- Understanding your course syllabus
- Taking notes in the college classroom
- Undecided? Picking a major

Yes, whether any of us want to admit it or not, the key to success in college life boils down to one simple and undeniable truth: We all have to go to our classes if we want to pass them and graduate. Despite what you might have heard about professors not caring whether you show up for class, *they do*. Remember, just because you sit in the back of the classroom does not mean that your professor won't notice it when you're always gone.

Academics should always be the main focus for anyone pursuing a higher education, not a second priority behind your social life. If you neglect your studies too often, you will end up riding alone down a poop creek without a paddle. Party too much, too hard, or even just on the wrong night, and you will quickly find that it can do terrible and irreparable damage to your grade-point average (especially if you are planning on attending graduate school, obtaining and/or retaining certain scholarships, or graduating with a 4.0 average). It's frightening, but true, that you could be dropped from a course with a grade of "F" for not showing up to class.

In this chapter, I focus on preparing for the long academic road that lies ahead. You'll see exactly why regular class attendance is so vitally important to your academic success, and what you need to do if you find that you cannot make it to class. The chapter also outlines the basic elements of your course syllabi—how to read them and, more important, how to understand and make use of them. In addition, you'll learn some effective and useful note-taking methods for college courses. Last, but certainly not least, I will offer you some guidelines on precisely how, and when you should choose a specific major that is right for you.

For the Love of All Things Good, Go to Class!

In just about every college classroom, there is going to be that one student who thinks that he or she can simply show up on the first day for roll call, then skip out on every class and just show up for the exams (or just come to class "when they feel like it"). Oddly enough, that person always seems to be the very same one who also acts shocked and dismayed when he or she shows up on exam day only to find that the professor has already removed his or her name from the class roster, assuming that he or she had dropped the class or left the school but forgotten to formally withdraw.

Professors are people, too—they are not telepathic mind readers. The responsibility of regular class attendance falls solely upon the individual student, and there is nothing that can be done to change the situation once a withdrawal has been done. You do not want to be that one student who gets the short end of the stick because you did not show up for class. Also remember that any professor has the absolute right to drop any student from a course with a final grade of "F" if that student accrues absences that the professor (or the university's absence policy) deems "excessive."

The Benefit of the Doubt

Even if you show up for class enough to finish the semester without getting dropped from the roster, it may still have an effect your final grade. I am not saying that a professor is going to give you a lower grade than you deserve (am I?), but he or she won't be inclined to do you any special favors, either.

For example, let's say for the sake of argument that your final average comes out to an 89—that breaks down to a letter grade of "B." However, you are also only one point away from an "A." Now, who do you think is the only person with the power to give you that point? That's right ... your professor! If the professor looks at your name and thinks, "I remember this student. That's the student who shows up every day and participates in class," then your chances of getting that grade-changing point are looking pretty good. On the other hand, if your professor looks at your name and thinks, "Who is this person? Were they even in my class?" If that happens, the odds are 99.99% that you are going to get stuck with your original letter grade of "B."

Campus Cautions

Normally, six or more absences in a semester will be grounds for a professor to drop a student from his or her course with a final grade of "F." Some professors might even have policies that call for disciplinary measures to be taken before six absences. For example, some professors might require an additional term paper (or worse) for any student with three or more absences.

Excused Absences

So what is a student *allowed* to be absent from class for? How do you know whether a day of missed classes is going to be counted as an excused absence? Traditionally, what are referred to as "excused" absences have been granted for any of the following situations:

- **Illness**—Unlike high school, you cannot get by with a note scribbled down by your mom. Usually, a doctor's note will be required upon your return for the absence to be counted as excused. If you are under the weather but can't get to a doctor, try to at least get verbal permission for missing class directly from your professor (and try to do it before class time).

- **Death in the family**—By all means, if a death has occurred back home, do not try to tough your way through it and miss a family funeral. It's as unhealthy as it is unnecessary. These days, universities are very understanding about this sort of thing, as long as it is someone either in your immediate family or at least close to it. Just inform your advisor and professors about the situation or, if you have to leave immediately, make sure that you have a trusted friend who can do it for you. If you are unable to find your professors in time, your advisor should see to it that you are granted excused absences and that your professors are informed of the situation (please, *do not* try to fake a death in the family … it's unethical and just bad form).

- **School-related athletics**—If you are an athlete on a school team (football, basketball, and so on), a cheerleader, or perhaps a marching band member, you will be excused for any missed class days due to playing/performing at these athletic events.

- **Scholastic conferences**—If you are representing your university at a scholars' conference or academic competition, then all that your professor will require of you is a dean's slip (the dean's office usually requires proof of attendance at the event, so make sure that you actually *go*) to be granted any excused absences that you might need. Before you spend any money on a conference, be sure that a dean's slip will be given or that you will not exceed the allowed number of absences.

Word, Yo!

Dean—a senior member of a college faculty who oversees administrative duties and the needs of the students in a particular department.

- **School-sponsored activities**—You will usually be excused from classes if you are going to be participating in any activity that is sponsored or hosted by your university such as an orientation, guest speaker's lecture, job fair, spirit rally, student organization fair, and so on. Participation counts as having a responsibility at the function, such as being an usher at a lecture or handling a booth at an organization fair. Simply *going* to the function will not be enough.

Word, Yo!

Excused absence—A missed class not counted against the student's class attendance record or final grade. Usually an absence must fall under specific criteria to be counted as "excused."

What Do You Do About Other Absences?

So what are you supposed to do in the case of an absence caused by an unforeseen emergency that does not fall under any of the mentioned categories? Don't go running after your professor in the hallway or interrupt his or her class just to explain why you were absent. All these things will accomplish is annoying your professor even further. (Just to reiterate a point made earlier in this book—annoying a professor is never a good idea!)

Your best bet is to simply explain the situation to your professor in person during his or her scheduled *office hours*, or call and make an appointment to speak with him or her at another time.

Word, Yo!

Office hours—Specifically scheduled days and times during the school week that professors have set aside for the purpose of meeting with their students for such things as term-paper seminars, counseling, and so on. If you need to see the professor outside office hours, he or she will require you to make an appointment

Understanding the All-Important Syllabus

A syllabus can be a big help in keeping up with your class work, papers, and assigned readings. Unfortunately, syllabi (plural for syllabus) can be confusing if you have never seen one before. Although syllabus formats vary by professor, the same basic information is available on every syllabus. As mentioned in Chapter 1, you should keep all your syllabi together in a specific folder to keep from losing, misplacing, or damaging them.

Here is the information that should be provided by your syllabus and why it is important:

- **Name of course professor, course call number, and course title/subject**—These items are on the syllabus to help you make sure you are not in the wrong class.

- **Time and place of professor's office hours**—The days and times that each professor will be available for private consultation with students, or office hours, should be provided. The professor might also include his or her preferred method for being seen by his/her students.

- **Professor's contact information**—Your professor's office telephone number, e-mail address, and any other contact information that he or she wishes to volunteer will be provided. Do not use any other method than those provided for contacting your professors.

- **Required textbooks and materials**—Your syllabus should list all of the items that will be required for each particular course—for example, textbooks, CD-ROMS, floppy disks, any specialized materials, pre-signed bluebooks, Scantron(s) to be handed in blank at the beginning of the semester, special calculators, rulers, and so on. When you go to purchase your textbooks, you should take your syllabus to the campus bookstore with you in order to prevent yourself from becoming confused and/or buying the wrong textbook. Three different professors may be teaching the same course but not using the same textbook.

- **Basic course outline/schedule**—The syllabus should include an approximate course schedule. This schedule lets you know what you need to read and when, how and when assignments are due and what they will be, the dates each quiz (pop quizzes excluded) and examination (including the final) will be given, as well as when class essays and term papers need to be handed in for a grade.

Bad Note-Taking + Not Reading = Bad Exam Scores

Unlike in high school, college professors are not required to tell you what information will be covered on quizzes and/or exams (and therefore usually don't and won't). This means that you are going to need to learn exactly how to take notes in such a way that you can use them to study effectively before a quiz or exam.

Not Just by the Book

Do not rely on your textbook as your one and only study guide. Although most of the information you need for a class *will* be in your textbook, many professors enjoy giving out necessary information during class lectures ... information that is *not* covered by the textbook. This is their special way of rewarding those students who always show up for class and of throwing a curve ball at those students who are never there. So yes ... you need to takes notes both from the textbook and from in-class lectures.

It Could Happen to You

I had this history professor once who did nothing but lecture. He never told us what we needed to know or write down ... so I never took any notes (in hindsight, that was really stupid of me). Then came the kicker. I studied the textbook before my first exam until I knew it like the back of my hand. Unfortunately, it turned out that the text was only *half* of the material on the exam. The rest of it was stuff he'd covered during in-class lectures ... stuff that I had never written down. I failed the first exam and spent the rest of the semester just struggling for a passing grade.

Jordan—Sophomore, UCLA

The TRAIL Note-Taking System

In order to take useful and effective notes, it will be helpful for you to remember the acronym *TRAIL*. TRAIL stands for *T*ext, *R*ead, *A*sk, *I*nvestigate, and *L*isten. TRAIL can be broken down into the five basic elements of good note-taking. Here is an explanation of these elements and how to properly exercise each of them:

- **Text**—While going over your assigned readings, it is always a good idea to write down each of the key terms from the textbook as you come across them. Most of the time, you can identify key terms by their appearance—showing up in the text as either **boldface type** or *in italics.* Once you have discovered a key term, find and write down the proper definition from either the textbook glossary or from another source (if the textbook does not include a glossary).

- **Read**—Try to familiarize yourself with your assigned readings *before* the day they are scheduled to be covered in the class lecture. This practice will prevent you from being completely in the dark on the subject the professor is lecturing on. You will be a step ahead of the next student and already have a basic understanding about what the lecture will cover. It will also help you to be prepared—allowing you to decide what questions to ask if the opportunity arises, as well as aid you in not looking like a dunce in the likely case that the professor unexpectedly confronts you with a question of his or her own.

- **Ask**—While there *is* such a thing as a stupid question, you will never know which questions are stupid unless you ask a lot of them. If you are confused about something, by all means raise your hand. If you do not understand something the professor has said, and are unable to interrupt the lecturer, ask some of your classmates who might have gotten the information down (but be sure to do this after class so that you do not get on the professor's bad side and disturb your classmates).

- **Investigate**—You will not always be fast enough on the draw to write out every single detail of a lecture on paper. Make sure that at the very least you get the main subject of what was said written down in your notes. For example, I write down a description of *Magna Carta* when my history professor mentions it, but he or she has already moved onto something new before I have time to write down the exact year it was signed. Obviously, this is something that I am going to need to find online or in the library later and add to my study notes. Investigate any parts of your notes that are incomplete until you have filled in all of the missing pieces.

- **Listen**—Professors will often change their tone of voice when mentioning something that students will need to know for an exam or quiz. Some professors will speak a decibel or so louder; others will say the information or term and then pause for a moment to give their students a chance to write it down. However, a professor will rarely ever say "you need to write this down." Listen closely to the way your professors speak. Try to get familiar with their lecture styles and changes in speech so that you can identify anything that indicates when important information is being given.

Polishing Your Notes

Before an exam—in fact, before you even plan to
start studying for an exam—it would behoove you
to collect your class notes and clean them up a bit.
This will make them more readable and therefore
easier to study. Some college students even go so
far as to type out their notes. You do not have to go
quite that far, but it definitely would not hurt anything if you did. Break your notes down into the
most necessary information. Remove any unnecessary information, scribbles, or personal notes as
you recopy them into your "study notes." This will
cut down on the amount of time it takes to sort
through your material as you study.

It's also always a good idea to compare notes with
another student in your class, just in case you
missed something that they perhaps did not. This
also benefits the other student for the very same
reason.

Trying to Make a "Major" Decision

I admit that choosing a major is probably one
of the toughest decisions for any college student
to make, but that's perfectly understandable. Obviously, picking a major seems like a pretty permanent thing ... deciding what you are going to "be
when you grow up," as we used to say as children
(heck, I still say it). In order to receive a degree,
however, we all will eventually have to choose a
specific field of study.

Undeclared—and Proud of It

As a college freshman, there is absolutely nothing wrong with not immediately declaring a major field of study. Many beginning college students start out their college careers as "undeclared" or "undecided," and there is nothing wrong with that. Your first year of classes will consist mainly of core requirement courses, anyway. None of those classes are major-specific—everyone has to take them.

So there is really no immediate reason for you to make a "major" decision. You have plenty of time to investigate the different majors that your university offers. As time goes on, you will start to develop a clearer idea of exactly which field of study is right for you.

Changing Your Mind and Your Major

Perceive choosing your major in the same way that you might perceive a dating relationship—you are not committed to anything until there is a wedding ring involved. In the same way, your major does not have to be permanent until you receive your degree. After you have chosen your field of study, should you for some reason feel that it might not be for you, or that you might be more comfortable in a different area, then you can always change it. So don't feel as though, because you have chosen a major, it is set in stone for all eternity. It is not, and you have every right to change your major as you see fit. This is going to affect your life and no one else's. Therefore, it should be your decision and no one has the right to stand in your way once you have made up your mind. You should, however, consider what others have to say.

Many university students decide to change their majors several times before finally receiving their degrees. Changing your major can make things more difficult, of course, depending on how big of a change it is. For example, switching from an English major/humanities minor to a humanities major/English minor will not cause your course requirements to change too drastically.

However, if you were to, say, change your field of study from a philosophy major to a business major, it could set back your graduation date by as much as a year because your course requirements are going to be extremely different. Some of the classes you've taken in the past will no longer count toward your degree, and there will be a lot of new classes required of you. As with anything in life, know what you're getting into before you take the plunge. Only an idiot tests the depth of water with both feet.

The main thing you need to avoid is changing your major drastically more than once. This not only takes a heavier toll on the total cost of your higher education, but it can cost you a heck of a lot more time. Seven years from now, you do not want to find yourself still in college working on a Bachelor's degree (do you?) just because you have changed your major 10 times. It has happened to students before, believe me. Don't let it happen to you.

Doubling Up

Feeling a little broad in the mind? Does one major not seem to be enough to cover your vast interests? Well, you can always "double up." Some students choose the double-major option for either this reason or because they have a split purpose—for example, a student who wants to work in the medical field but has an interest in education might have a pre-med major coupled with an education major (such a degree might help them prepare to be a health-care educator later in life).

A double major can mean a much larger workload, however, and may make the road to graduation much longer. Due to this, you should thoroughly investigate your decision as well as consult with your staff advisor before choosing this option (or making any other decisions regarding your major).

The Least You Need to Know

- Class attendance can have an impact your grades—a negative impact if you are constantly absent.
- Keep track of your syllabi and know how to read as well as understand them.
- *TRAIL*—Textbook, Read, Ask, Investigate, and Listen—are the five essentials of effective note-taking.
- Don't feel that you have to rush when deciding on a major. Take your time, look around, and know what you are getting into.

- Remember that while a major can be changed, doing so too often or too drastically can postpone your graduation date and increase your workload.

How Am I Going to Study in All This Chaos?

In This Chapter

- Making time to study
- Cramming for tests
- Forming a study group
- Pulling an "all-nighter"

Between attending classes and lectures, and dealing with exams, essays, and assigned readings, how in the world are you ever going to find enough time to study? And even when you do find the time, where on this great green earth are you supposed to go when the library is completely full and your roommate is blasting his stereo system so loud that you swear your ears will bleed for days?

This chapter focuses on studying—study methods, how to make time for study, and how to do it effectively. I will teach you exactly how to make time for yourself to study, along with providing you some suggestions on alternative study locations

and methods, just in case the usual ones are un-
available for whatever reason (it happens). I will
also talk about some of the basic pros and cons of
using cram-session study methods for your exam
preparation. I show you how to go about rallying
some of your fellow classmates together to form
a study group, and suggest some methodology on
how to conduct one. I will also discuss the ins and
outs of the traditional "all-nighter" study session—
just how and when you should hold one, as well as
how and when you should *not* hold one.

If You Don't *Have* Time to Study ... *Make* Time to Study

You cannot study if your schedule is so full that you
don't have a free moment in the day. This can be a
real obstacle for any college student, especially for
those who are working to pay tuition costs and living expenses. Unfortunately, acknowledging the
fact that you have more on your plate than you
should does not change your situation a bit. Even
if you don't have any time to study, you still have to
do it. But how? Well, as ridiculous as this sounds,
you have to *make* time.

How in the world do you make time? Well, making
time means working your study time into other
activities. Here are some examples:

- Keep a Xerox copy of your notes next to the
  toilet and read them while you're doing
  your business (hey, it works).

- If you have a lunch break at work, study your list of key terms (see Chapter 6).

- Do you have a lot of appointments that are cutting into your time? Well, I have found that a waiting room can be a better place to study than a library (because everyone is so quiet ... why is that?).

- Anytime you sit down to eat can be a perfect opportunity for you to peruse your notes, which by now you know will be your main resource of studying for exams (or at least, you *should*).

As a matter of fact, any idle moment is a study opportunity—bus rides, bathroom breaks, lunch breaks, waiting rooms, long lines (like at the DMV/DPS), between classes, and so on, are all places of opportunity for the college student on-the-go to wedge in some study time. For more on how to manage your time more effectively, see Chapter 11.

Although the above-mentioned methods of study are not what anyone would call "preferred methods," you at least have to admit that some study time is better than no study time at all. However, if you use these methods regularly (and not just right before an exam), they will greatly improve your chances of maintaining your grades in the face of an already-busy daily schedule.

It Could Happen to You

Unlike a lot of students I know, no one paid my way through my undergrad years of college. I had to work my rear off to get my Bachelor's degree. I worked two jobs and went to school full time. I studied during every free moment. Looking back, I don't know how I managed to do as well as I did. Now that I'm a grad student, the school is "paying my way." I never realized how much easier studying would be if I only had the time.

Anonymous—Graduate Assistant, University of New Mexico

The Pros and Cons of "Cramming"

For as long as there have been institutions of learning in the world, there have probably also been cram sessions. Cramming is when a student does all of his or her studying on the evening immediately preceding the exam. Due to laziness, procrastination, or bad planning, something went awry and now he or she is like a football player facing game day while still trying to locate his or her helmet. Cramming is the only option the student has left. May the heavens have pity on these poor souls, because their professors most certainly will not.

There is not necessarily anything wrong with cramming, as long as it is not the only study method that you are using. Cramming should be done in association with another more regular study schedule. For example, if you have taken even one night a week for studying over the course of the semester, cramming can be a great way to review all of the necessary information. However, if you find that you are cramming simply because you have not even looked at your notes since you wrote them down … it might not be enough to save you, and you really should have found a better way (but it's too late for that now).

Word, Yo!

Cramming—also referred to as "*cram sessions*"; a study method consisting of a student trying to absorb as much information as possible on the evening immediately preceding the exam. The name is meant to describe how the student is trying to "cram" as much relevant information into his or her head as possible.

In order to avoid finding yourself cornered into the terror-stricken panic that is a "cram session," you should be studying regularly throughout the entire semester. If you set aside a weekly study period, as mentioned earlier, it will not only help you to avoid cramming altogether, but will improve the quality and the amount of time it takes for your final study periods. If however, you cannot or will not do this, here are some tips on how to cram for a test:

- Concentrate on your list of key terms in your notes.

- For literature classes, buy *Cliff's Notes* so that you can at least go over the most essential elements of the books that you were supposed to have already read.

 Word, Yo!

Comprehensive examination—a final exam that consists of questions which are relative to all of the material covered throughout an entire course. Unlike a final exam, which deals with the last information covered, a comprehensive exam deals with all of the previously tested information as well.

- Try to find a study group of classmates who will also be cramming. Several minds are better than one, usually. (See the next section for how to form a study group.)

- See if your professor is willing to meet with you during office hours and give you some idea as to what needs to be studied for the exam (although this does not always work, and sometimes it even backfires ... so be careful).

- Focus the attention of your study on any terms or concepts that have been mentioned more than once throughout the course.

- If you know anyone who has taken the same course you are taking and, if possible, with the same professor, probe that student's mind for any helpful hints that might be of use, such as key concepts, the exam's main focus, and so on.

 It Could Happen to You

I never studied for tests when I was in high school, so why should college be any different? Well, I found out the hard way. In college, nobody is there to hold your hand or make sure that you know the material, or even [tell you] what you should study.

Jason—Sophomore, University of North Texas

As mentioned, you should in no way consider cramming to be a preferred or even favorable study method. If anything, you should think of cramming as either supplemental to a regular study schedule or as a last-ditch effort to prepare (because you are obviously unprepared). Have a regular study schedule and take the stress out of your study time—you will feel much better.

A Call to Arms: Forming Study Groups

Any experienced college student will tell you that study groups are one of the best ways to prepare for exams. Not only are study groups better because they pull together the minds and information of several students, but also because they allow students to practice *"question-and-answer"* (*Q&A*) study methods. A study group also helps to keep everyone focused on the task at hand and reduces the chances of forgetting to study necessary material.

Word, Yo!

Question-and-answer (Q&A)—a study method consisting of two or more students quizzing one another on material that will likely be a part of an upcoming exam. An example Q&A technique is the use of flash cards.

Who to Include

Before you run off and start pulling together other students at random, however, there are a few things you may want to consider. First of all, you should think about exactly what kind of students would be most beneficial to a study group (this does not mean the students you think will be the most fun to have around, necessarily). For example, the class

clown might not be the best choice to invite into
your study group. He might be funny, but constant
joking will only become another unnecessary distraction. As with any cooperative/team activity, a
chain is only as strong as its weakest link. Try to
avoid inviting any potential "weak links" into your
group. Anyone who might be distracting or in any
way disruptive of the flow of work is not a good
candidate for invitation into a study group.

You'll want to try to get the movers and shakers,
the thinkers and brains, among your classmates to
join your group. These are the students who participate in class discussions, always seem to know
the answer to what is asked during lectures, and
always show up for class. Why in the world would
you want to invite the guy who sits at the very back
of the class, flirting with every girl in sight, into
your group? Do you honestly think that he is going
to contribute to the whole, or do you think he'll
just take whatever information he needs and free-
load off of everyone else? In most cases, it will
prove to be the latter.

What if you don't exactly have the kind of charisma
or commanding presence to make joining your
group appealing to other students? Well, remember that free stuff (namely, free *food*) is always a
good lure.

Group Study Tips

Even with well-selected students, an unorganized
study group, unfortunately, can sometimes do more

harm than good. Therefore, it is important for whomever is hosting the group to already have an idea of how the group will be conducted.

One of the best methods for studying with a group by Q&A is to make some flash cards. Simply go to the store and buy some 3 " × 5 " ruled note cards. On the blank side of each card, write down a key term or concept—make sure that you write it large enough to be read from across a table. Turn the card over on its flip side (the ruled side) and write out the definition/explanation of the term or concept. In this way, the group will be able to work together more effectively and efficiently.

A little creativity can help to make the study group interesting as well as beneficial. The best way to make studying more fun is by turning it into a contest or making a game of it. Flash cards are great for creating games. Here are some examples of study games you can do with flash cards:

- In each round, one person has the cards and everyone else answers questions. The first person to get a question wrong must take the cards, shuffle them, and begin again. You can vary this any way you like.

- Another game is for each person to draw the same number of flash cards (a good rule of thumb is seven cards per person, but make sure all of the cards in the deck are being played). Then go around in one direction and have students try to stump each other with the questions. The asker can ask any question in his or her hand to any player they choose. If someone does not know the answer to a question, they must take the card. If they answer correctly, however, the asker must now take a card from whoever gave that answer. Whoever runs out of cards first wins.

It Could Happen to You

I do not know what I would do without my study groups. My schedule is so busy that I usually only have time to schedule one long study session before each exam. A few hours of studying with a group seems about equal to several weeks of study, I think. Quizzing each other on the stuff that will be on the exam is a big help. Sometimes, we'll even have a few questions that are nearly identical to questions that end up being on the actual exam. I suggest study groups to anyone who has the means.

Anonymous—Senior, Midwestern State University

Remember that although a study group can be a lot of fun, it is meant for *study*. Even though study groups are social in nature, they are in no way a social function. Conversation is great, but not if it starts cutting into your study time. Do your best to keep your group focused. If a member of the group seems to be causing distractive problems, do not invite them back.

All-Nighters? Only If You Can Sleep the Next Day

Like cramming, an all-night study session can be great when done in association with a regular study schedule. However, all-nighters are not and should not be used as last-minute cramming sessions right before an exam. This is not going to help you much. An all-night study session should be done on a night when you can get at least eight hours of sleep (see Chapter 2) afterward.

The Main Reason Not to Study All Night

Do not, I repeat *do not* attempt to pull off an all-night study session on the evening immediately preceding your exam. Trust me, it's not worth the pain. All that this will do is make you tired, cranky, and exhausted for your exam. All of the cramming and reading in the world is not going to help you once you have started taking a test and are running on less than two hours of sleep. If you look around the room just before the professor starts handing out the exams, you can tell which students were up all night studying—they are the pale ones with bags under their eyes, their faces resting on one hand as their eyes continually close and open like a faulty garage door.

The Right Way to All-Night It

However, if you are just itching to go all-out, all night long, and are willing to do it as I have suggested, then get some coffee, some snacks, and whatever vices you need for the night (nicotine, sodas, whatever). Go find yourself a comfortable spot and settle in for several hours of information download.

Once your eyes start to get tired and begin to droop closed (or if, say, the sun starts coming up), you will know it is time to go home and crash. Once your mind has gone into the "I want to take a nap" mode, all you are really doing is staring blankly at a textbook, anyway, and possibly hurting your eyes. You are no longer absorbing any information, so why keep pushing your way toward futility? Remember that study and sleep should go together like Scantrons and No. 2 pencils … one will not work without the other.

Staying Awake for an All-Nighter (or Anytime You're Studying)

You might find that staying awake to study all night is a lot harder than you thought. Sometimes, the harder we try to stay conscious, the more difficult it becomes. However, nodding off is not going to help with your studying. Here are some helpful tips on staying awake and staying alert. These tips are suggestions, of course, and you should do whatever works best for you (as long as it does work).

- **Drink water**—Drinking water is a great way to keep yourself awake. Even today's U.S. Marines use this strategy for keeping alert during the exhausting schedule of boot camp. Water contains oxygen, which gives the body a little shot of alertness.

- **Slap to the back of the head**—I know, it sounds kind of silly, but it does work. Not an extremely hard slap, but enough to give you a little sting. This is much more effective than the old slap-in-the-face method. You can slap yourself, or have someone else do it for you.

- **Caffeine**—Let's hear it for old reliable! Unfortunately, this old standby also comes with a drawback: It dehydrates your body and can cause even more fatigue once its effects have worn off. This, of course, requires you to consume even more caffeine. Try to steer clear of caffeine pills or ephedrine-loaded supplements. Stick to coffee; it's safer (you never hear of anyone dying from an accidental coffee overdose).

- **Stretching**—When you feel yourself starting to become fatigued, stand up for a moment and reach for the ceiling. You can also stretch by clasping your hands together behind your back and pushing them up and out, expanding your chest and straightening your posture. Sitting hunched over a desk or book can be murder on your back. Not only is stretching good for your spine, but it helps with your body's circulation, therefore increasing your level of alertness.

- **Take a short walk**—Get up and take a brief walk outside or just around the room. Get out and take a breath of fresh air (or the opposite if you are a smoker). Just getting your body moving and the blood circulating can be an effective method for staying awake. This is a great choice because it helps you to avoid the lulling affect of being stationary for an extended period of time.

The Least You Need to Know

- Just because you do not have the time to study, does not mean that you can't *make* the time to study.
- Cram sessions should be a supplemental form of study, not your *sole* form of study.
- Study groups are a very beneficial way to study for exams. Whenever possible, join or form a study group for your classes.
- All-nighters can be fun, but don't pull one on the evening immediately preceding an exam.

Chapter 8

Let's Talk About Sex!

In This Chapter

- Safe sexual activity and sexually transmitted diseases
- Unplanned pregnancy
- How to avoid rape (and what to do if it happens to you)

Dating ... sex ... relationships ... with all the academic stress that we experience in college, the last thing that any of us needs is to have even more unnecessary stress tacked onto us by our personal lives. During college, for probably the first time in your life, your parents will no longer be an issue in your personal life and/or sexual decisions. You'll have the freedom to do a lot of the things that you could not (or were not allowed to do) back home. This freedom also opens the door for you to become sexually active (if you have not already). As with any new experience, there are risks to sexual activity.

In this chapter, we brave the tempestuous waters of the romantic interpersonal relationships ... a dangerous venture for any human being (just read *Romeo and Juliet*). I discuss the ins and outs (no pun intended) of being sexually active. As uncomfortable as this may be for either one of us ... we do have to talk about it. The chapter covers sexually transmitted diseases and unplanned pregnancies and how to safely avoid them. I will also discuss the issue of date rape (and the subject of rape in general)—what legally defines a rape, how to avoid risky situations that can lead to being date raped, and what to do if (heaven forbid) this were to happen to you or any of your friends.

Don't Catch Anything You Can't Wash Off: Safe Sex

Let's try to get the most painful part of this chapter over with right from the start: Sexually Transmitted Diseases (or STDs). According to information posted by the Centers for Disease Control (CDC), "The surest way to avoid transmission of sexually transmitted diseases is to abstain from sexual intercourse or to be in a long-term mutually monogamous relationship with a partner who has been tested and you know is uninfected." Obviously, not everyone is able or willing to follow this advice. For those readers, I provide the following information.

The Condom: Not Just a Really Sturdy Water Balloon

The most commonly recommended method for the prevention of STDs (as well as unplanned/unwanted pregnancies) is the use of the male latex condom, preferably one with a spermicidal lubricant. While the CDC claims that condoms coated with spermicidal lubricants are no more effective against the transmission of STDs than are normal latex condoms with nonspermicidal lubrication, spermicidal lubricants are still more effective in the prevention of unwanted pregnancy (something that can be a lot more permanent than some STDs).

 Word, Yo!

Spermicide—a special substance, normally found on condoms in the form of a lubricant, designed to kill living sperm before they can cause conception, or pregnancy.

Of course, condoms are not 100 percent effective (nothing is, aside from abstinence) in preventing the transmission of STDs or preventing unwanted pregnancy. However, it is common knowledge that the correct and consistent use of male latex condoms can significantly reduce the risks of both pregnancy and STDs. Here are the facts on both male and female (yes, they have those now) latex condoms:

- **Male latex condoms**—Male latex condoms, when used properly and consistently, are approximately 98 percent effective in preventing the spread of HIV/AIDS and other sexually transmitted diseases. Although they are not 100 percent effective, this does not mean that they do not work. Nor does this mean that they should not be used. Gentlemen, please protect yourself and others by learning how to *properly* put one on (Tip #1: Don't open a condom with your teeth). There is no shame in reading the instructions pamphlet that is enclosed in every package of condoms. Incorrect use of a condom can seriously compromise its integrity as a contraceptive and as a protective measure against disease/infection. Ladies, there is no shame in learning to put a condom on a guy! If he won't do it, then you should!

- **Female latex condoms**—Finally, modern technology has decided to catch up with the independent female. Although, of course, there is no reason that a woman cannot carry male condoms with her when she plans on participating in sexual intercourse, she now has the choice to carry her own form of protection. Studies do vary, however, on the effectiveness of the female latex condom—findings range from as low as 80 percent to as high as 95 percent effectiveness. The general consensus remains, however, that the male condom is more effective than the female condom (which is still being modified and fine-tuned in certain respects).

Although condoms are not the only method available to you, they are the most highly recommended. Obviously, there are other forms of contraceptives available, but most only prevent pregnancy and few are for the prevention of STD transmission. Remember that someone who does not have enough love and respect (be it a man or a woman) to protect the both of you, is not someone worth risking your life over. There should be no excuse that a lover could use to talk you out of using one.

Sexually Transmitted Diseases Don't Wash Off

Remember that every time you sleep with someone, you are also sleeping with everyone they have had sex with in the past (as far as STDs are concerned, of course). Think about this before putting your life and/or your future at risk.

Now that we have discussed the use of the condom, let's take a moment to talk a little bit about the alternative to protection ... infection. It is a nasty subject, I realize, but you need to know about it ... everyone needs to know about it. The truth is that ignorance about STDs is sometimes the real killer. Some people who become infected do not know what is happening to them and do not go to see the doctor out of fear, sometimes delaying medical attention until it's too late to be treated. Don't risk insanity, disfigurement, or death over something that can be treated easily with antibiotics. No amount of shame or embarrassment is worth your life.

Survival of the Cheapest

A package of three male latex condoms can cost anywhere from $4 to $8 retail. However, most university clinics (as well as just about any local health department) give them out free and with no questions asked. So not being able to afford them is no excuse ... neither is being embarrassed (no one is going to laugh at you). Free protection is out there and it is not hard to find, so take advantage of it. If you are unsure about where, make an anonymous call to the campus clinic and inquire about when and where you can get free condoms.

In order to aid you in identifying STD infection, the following list details some of the most commonly encountered sexually transmitted diseases. First, here are some STDs that are currently without cures. Catch one of these and you will have it for the rest of your life:

- **HIV/AIDS**—HIV (which stands for Human Immunodeficiency Virus) is the name used to refer to the virus that in time turns into full-blown AIDS (short for Acquired Immune Deficiency Syndrome). Someone who is already infected with another sexually transmitted disease is at an increased risk of acquiring AIDS. HIV/AIDS can remain dormant in the host for as long as 6 months after initial infection. This means that you could test negative even though you actually have the disease. Sadly, there is currently no known cure for AIDS, and it is 100 percent fatal.

- **Herpes**—Herpes simplex virus (HSV) normally comes in two types: genital and oral. It is estimated that roughly 30 million Americans currently have the herpes simplex form of the virus. Unfortunately, there is only one surefire way to be certain that you have genital herpes … after you already have a sore. There is no known cure for herpes; however, there is medication available to control outbreaks of sores. Despite rumors you may hear, it is quite possible to transmit herpes even when no symptoms are present, and there are many who are infected with the herpes virus who do not show any symptoms.

The following are some commonly contracted STDs that are curable with antibiotics. If you show symptoms or suspect that you have been infected/exposed to any of them, seek medical attention as soon as you possibly can:

- **Chlamydia**—Chlamydia is the most commonly contracted sexually transmitted disease. Five percent of women are infected with chlamydia. Seventy-five percent of infected women do not show symptoms, nor do 25 percent of men. If you wait too long to seek medical attention, chlamydia can lead to pelvic inflammatory disease in women, and possibly sterility. It is possible to pass chlamydia on to babies during delivery. In infants this disease can lead to pneumonia, eye infections, and even permanent blindness. Chlamydia is tested for during most standard STD testing.

- **Gonorrhea**—Over 1 million cases of gonorrhea are reported each year in the United States alone. This disease can result in sterility, arthritis, and cardiovascular problems. In females, it can cause pelvic inflammatory disease and stillbirth. It has been known to cause blindness in newborns. Common symptoms are a yellow to green vaginal discharge in women, or a puss-like discharge in men. Eighty percent of infected women and 10 percent of infected men show no symptoms.

- **Syphilis**—Untreated, syphilis can result in some pretty nasty stuff—brain damage, disfigurement, madness, and eventually death. Symptoms are visible sores. This STD is most contagious when sores are visible, although it can be transmitted anytime during an infection. Syphilis can also result in stillbirths and birth defects, as well as blindness in infants.

- **Pubic lice**—Otherwise known as "crabs." Symptoms include painful itching around the genital or rectal area, fever, and unusual fatigue. Pubic lice can be spread by more than just sexual contact—infested bed sheets, clothing, and furniture are also possible mediums for catching these critters. Pubic lice can be treated with any standard lice treatment available on the market, such as Nix or RID.

- **Genital warts (HPV)**—These annoying and very contagious sores have to be frozen off with nitrogen. You can imagine how painful that might be. They also never completely go away, and will reoccur for the rest of your life.

It Could Happen to You _____

I never thought I'd get HIV. I never imagined it. I thought HIV and AIDS only happened to addicts and prostitutes. I never liked condoms. I thought that as long as I avoided druggies and hookers I was safe. Well, I learned the hard way how wrong I was. The girl who infected me was as clean as they come. Two years ago, she died of full-blown AIDS. She was 25 years old. I just turned 23 this year ... and am wondering when my time will come. Don't cut your life short. It's not worth the fear and pain that I deal with on a daily basis. It's a nightmare.

Anonymous—University Senior (School name withheld to protect privacy)

Oh, Baby! Unplanned Pregnancy

Another risk of sexual activity is, of course, pregnancy. First and foremost, whether or not you are in a monogamous, exclusive relationship, an unplanned or unwanted pregnancy can easily bring your college education plans to an abrupt and unpleasant end. Remember that even though an unplanned pregnancy can be terminated, it can never be reversed. This section assumes that you and your partner are unwilling or unable to stay together and care for a baby.

In recent years, abortion has become a somewhat more acceptable (or at least legalized) method for terminating an unwanted pregnancy. However, due to the health risks that are involved (mentally as well as physically) with having an abortion, you may want to consider other options should you find yourself (or your girlfriend, if you are a male) unexpectedly pregnant. Remember, if you are pregnant, it is your body and the choice is yours to make … no one else should make you feel as if they have the right to make it for you.

The Dangers of Abortion*

The leading causes of abortion-related fatalities are hemorrhaging, infection, embolisms, anesthesia problems, and undiagnosed ectopic pregnancy. Legal abortion has been reported as the fifth leading cause of maternal fatalities in the United States. It might be even more due to the suspected number of unreported deaths.

Women with one abortion face a moderately higher risk of developing cervical cancer as opposed women who have not. Women with two or more abortions face a significantly higher risk. Approximately 3 percent of all abortion patients suffer a perforation of the uterus. This injury can remain undiagnosed, and therefore, untreated.

*Author's Note: Certain data has been adapted from information published by The Elliot Institute in Springfield IL, the American Journal of Ob & Gyn, and The Journal of The American Medical Association (JAMA).

Damage to your uterus can result in complications with pregnancies later in your life and could quite possibly evolve into problems that can require you to have a hysterectomy. You might not want a baby right now, but that shouldn't endanger your chances of having one in the future. One day ... who knows what you might want?

It Could Happen to You

My friend almost died after getting an abortion. After one of those home tests came up positive, her boyfriend just shoved some money in her hands and told her to go get one. She went all by herself without telling anyone. She didn't even have a friend take her home afterward. She just got in a cab. It wasn't long after she got home that she saw the bleeding was not stopping. In fact, it was getting worse. She passed out in her bathroom. Her mom found her just in time to call 911 and save her stupid #*$. No one else knew that she was even pregnant, except for her boyfriend. She could have died ... and for what?

Anonymous—School and Class Withheld

Alternatives to Having an Abortion

Before you make a final decision to do something as permanent and risky as aborting your pregnancy, you may want to consult with a Planned Parenthood counselor first to see what type of options are available.

Campus Cautions

If a crisis counselor is not available on your university campus, most urban areas (especially those near college campuses) have some form of unplanned-pregnancy center available off campus. Sometimes these centers are supported by the funding of state health departments, while others run on private donations. It is always better to be well-informed about every option of any major decision before you make it … how to deal with an unplanned pregnancy is no different. Seek out all the guidance, input, and information that you possibly can before deciding on the best method for dealing with an unplanned conception.

The following are also some of the most recently available alternative methods for dealing with an unwanted pregnancy:

- **Adoption**—This is becoming an increasingly popular choice for unready or unwed mothers. Instead of terminating a pregnancy, you can give your baby to a couple that is ready, willing, and able to care for an infant. Many college campuses across the country now have a student crisis center in some form that can help you to find a suitable couple for adopting your baby. Your medical costs will likely be completely covered by the adopting couple.

- **"No-Questions-Asked" Turn In at a Hospital**—Some states have decided to put a "no-questions-asked" policy into action at certain hospitals in order to curb the frequency of situations where babies have died after being abandoned in unsuitable locations (such as dumpsters and doorsteps) and not found in time. All one needs to do is bring the baby to the hospital and turn him or her in. Make sure that your state has this policy before you attempt this.

- **The Morning-After Pill**—Also known as Emergency Contraception (E.C.). These contraceptive pills have been used with much success in Europe and other countries for quite some time. The pills contain hormones that hold up ovulation, inhibit the fertilization process, or make it impossible for a fertilized egg to attach to the uterus. They contain almost the same hormones as regular birth control pills, but in much higher doses. If taken within 72 hours after having sexual intercourse (as in "the morning after," hence the nickname of the pill) they might counter potential conception. As of this year, the Planned Parenthood program offers prescriptions for E.C. over the internet. However, this is only in certain states. Many family-planning and college health clinics dispense these pills as well.

The side effects of the morning-after pill can include nausea, vomiting, and tenderness in the breasts. E.C. pills should not be considered as substitutes for other forms of birth control, i.e. condoms or daily birth control pills. E.C. pills can be a bit expensive, as well—anywhere from $20 to $30 for a single dose. For goodness' sake, don't forget that these pills still don't protect you from sexually transmitted diseases.

The Worst Crime Against Another Human Being: Rape

In recent years, rape has ceased to be the silent evil that it once was. Even more, *date rape* and *acquaintance rape* are receiving more and more acknowledgment each year. It is a sad fact that many rapes are perpetrated by an assailant who knows the victim. By basic definition, rape is any form of sexual intercourse or contact that is done without the mutual consent of all parties involved.

There is never any reason or excuse that can justify raping someone. Nor is there any reason that a victim of rape should be made to feel that it is his/her fault. The act of rape is both cowardly and immoral, not to mention illegal.

It Could Happen to You

I thought rapes only happened to girls. I never imagined it could happen to me. After all, I'm a strong guy. And strong guys ... don't get raped. Yeah, right. That night, some guys slipped enough ecstasy into my drink to put me into an incoherent daze. I didn't even know what had happened until it was too late. To this day, I've never told anyone and I've never reported it to the police. I've been an idiot. Now I'm in therapy being treated for Post-Traumatic Stress Disorder. Don't do what I did. It wasn't your fault.

Anonymous—Sophomore, Midwestern State University

What to Do If You Have Been Raped

If you have been raped, here are some guidelines to follow in order to ensure that the police will be able to prosecute your attacker:

- Do not take a shower or bathe. Many rape victims are psychologically traumatized and feel an urge to wash themselves clean; however, this can destroy precious evidence.

- Call the police right away. Try to have a description of your assailant and vehicle if possible.

- Get to the emergency room or call an ambulance immediately. In the latter case, tell the 911 operator that you have been raped so that the EMS vehicle brings a rape kit. A rape kit is used to collect forensic/ DNA evidence to ensure prosecution and conviction of a suspect. This evidence also prevents accidental misidentification.

- Seek rape crisis counseling and attempt to find a support group as soon as you are able.

An Ounce of Prevention

To avoid needing to take these measures, here are some tips on how to stay away from high-risk situations:

- Avoid blind dates.

- If you plan to go on a blind date, meet this person in a public place and take your own car.

- Never get into a car with someone you do not know.

- Never bring home or go to the home of someone you do not know.

- Never accept a drink from someone you do not know. (See Chapter 9 for more about GHB, the "date-rape drug.")

- If you leave a drink unattended, do not drink from it again … go get a new one.

Whether you choose to follow any or none of the guidelines suggested, it is important to understand this: Rape is not the fault of the victim! It is a mind game for weak sick-o-paths who are too cowardly to stand up to their own shadows. Never allow them to victimize you more than they already have by believing that in some way you allowed this to happen. You did not.

The Least You Need to Know

- Protect yourself from sexually transmitted diseases and pregnancy by using a condom or just not having sex.

- Know the facts about and alternatives to abortion.

- Know how to avoid becoming a rape victim. But if it happens to you, report it.

Alcohol, Spirits, Brain Grenades, and the Morning After

In This Chapter

- Alcohol do's and don'ts
- Drugs and drug abuse
- GHB—why it's unethical and illegal

Alcohol … whether or not anyone wants to admit it, it's a part of the college experience. So are drugs. As with many things you'll encounter in college, no one is going to stop you from drinking. Therefore, the control must come from within. If you choose to drink (and you probably will), then it's important for you to know how to do it responsibly, safely, and correctly. Otherwise, you might wake up in the parking lot of a public park, naked in the backseat of your car, with someone else's underwear tied around your head and no idea how you got there (don't ask). This chapter will help you avoid embarrassing situations such as these (or at least cut down on their frequency).

In this chapter, I will be talking about alcohol, in all its varied and wondrous forms; and drugs, what they are, and what they can do to you. I will cover the subjects of DWI arrests, alcohol poisoning, and the dangers of a drug overdose. I might not be able to stop you from consuming drugs and alcohol, but I can at least educate you and prepare you to face them like a champ. And remember, it might always be five o'clock somewhere ... but that does not make it five o'clock here, and it never will.

Don't Become a Priest of the Porcelain Temple

No one likes to hang out with someone that they are going to be stuck babysitting every time he or she starts to drink. It's important to know your limitations so that you don't end up with your head in a toilet. Remember ... being drunk may be fun, but being sick as a dog is very much the opposite. And the line between these two can be crossed very quickly.

How Much Can You Tolerate?

Everyone reacts to alcohol differently, based on a few key physiological factors. These factors can either slow down or speed up the effects of alcohol on an individual's system. Pay attention because,

unlike algebra, you'll probably have to use this
information someday:

- **Weight**—The more you weigh, the higher
  your tolerance; and the less you weigh, the
  lower your tolerance. For example, a six
  pack of beer might not be much for a 200-
  pound person, but it can be a lot for someone who weighs 120 pounds or less.

- **Gender**—Some studies have shown that
  alcohol affects females faster than it does
  males. However, some correlation has been
  found in the weight ratios (see above)
  between men and women—men normally
  being the heavier of the two. For example, a
  180-pound male will have a higher tolerance
  than a 100-pound female.

- **Food consumption**—Be aware of whether
  you have eaten before you start to drink. It's
  a very bad idea to consume alcohol on an
  empty stomach, especially hard liquor. Not
  only will the alcohol enter your bloodstream
  faster, but drinking when you have not eaten
  in more than a few hours will also increase
  your chances of getting sick. In some cases,
  this also increases your risk of alcohol poisoning.

- **Genetics**—For some reason, some people
  are born with a naturally high or low tolerance for alcohol. If you're brave, you might
  want to inquire to your parents about this
  (or not). They could tell you whether there

are any genetic factors you should be aware of—including alcoholism. If you have a family history of alcoholism, your chances of becoming an alcoholic are extremely high. You might want to consider this before you take a drink.

Word, Yo!

Porcelain God—also referred to as **The Temple of the Porcelain God**. This is a slang term referring to a toilet, usually in the context that someone who has had too much drink is on his or her knees in front of it, or hanging on it, because he or she is puking up his or her stomach lining. Because the drunken individual is in a kneeling position, he or she resembles a person in prayer, hence the term.

A good rule of thumb for consuming alcohol without getting completely wasted is to have no more than one drink every hour. One drink means one 12-ounce beer, glass of wine, or shot of hard liquor. No matter which way you slice it, they all have the same amount of alcohol in them. If you suddenly find that you have lost track of how many drinks you've had or when you had your last drink, just park your car and lose your keys. Congratulations, you are officially drunk.

The Fine Print

Another quick subject before we move on: legalities. Not that this is going to stop some of you, but at least you will have been warned. In the United States, you must be 21 years of age to legally consume alcohol. If you are not 21 and are caught drinking, you will most likely get ticketed for an MIP (Minor In Possession of a controlled substance). It's not too serious, but it does require a court appearance, and your parents will not be too happy when they are notified.

Also, most states have a blood-alcohol-content (BAC) limit of no more than .05, although in some places it is still .08. If you are pulled over and blow past the legal limit, you will be arrested for Driving While Intoxicated (DWI). A DWI comes with its own myriad costs, penalties, and other assorted pains in the backside. Depending on where you live, multiple DWIs can be a felony and you will end up in jail.

You don't want a DWI, so here is the best way to avoid them. When you go somewhere that you will be drinking, plan on staying or have enough money to get a cab. Trust me, it's cheaper than the alternative.

Alcohol Poisoning: Yes, It Can Happen to Anyone

Alcohol poisoning is probably one of the best reasons I can offer you for paying attention to the drinking guidelines I mentioned earlier. Most people believe that the worst you can get from drinking too much is a miserable night paying homage to the porcelain god and a head full of pain the next morning. Nobody ever thinks about dying from it. But it can happen … it has happened and it does happen all the time.

Survival of the Cheapest

Due to some of the recent changes in the law, which hold the bars responsible for those who leave there drunk, many bars will now get you a *free cab* if you just tell them that you are too drunk to drive. But even if they don't, it's no excuse for driving drunk.

The human body can only take so much. As with anything else, too much alcohol is a bad thing. That's why you get sick when you drink too much. Your body is telling you to stop. However, I have seen guys go puke their guts out and then turn around only to chug down another beer bong. Alcohol kills brain cells and depresses the body, slowing down even involuntary functions such as your heart rate. Too much alcohol can send you into cardiac arrest. And after your bloodstream has absorbed a lethal amount, there is little that even a stomach pump can do for you.

Keep this thought in your mind when you think about taking your friend up on a challenge of lined-up tequila shots: It could quite possibly kill one of you. Who cares which one of you can drink the most without puking? Is it really worth your life? Besides, once you have that much tequila, that party is pretty well over for the both of you, isn't it? Neither of you is going to remember who won anyway, so why put your lives in jeopardy?

It Could Happen to You

Growing up, I always heard my old man joke about "Going ten rounds with Jose Cuervo." It always sounded like so much fun when he'd tell stories about it. When I finally tried to do this myself after I left home for college, I learned the hard way why he bragged about it so much. I barely got through round eight before I was hugging a toilet groaning "never again." Well … never say "never again," because I have attempted several times to make it to ten. Hasn't happened yet.

Anonymous—sophomore, Midwestern State University

A One-Way Ticket to Veggie-Ville: Drugs and Drug Abuse

If you haven't already been exposed to drugs, you will definitely see them once or twice when you get to college. My advice? Steer clear of them. As Mr. Mackey would say, "Drugs are bad," not to mention illegal and dangerous. Chances are, however, most of you are not going to follow that advice. So as usual, I will help you prepare for that which I can't stop you from doing.

The Usual Suspects

Here is a list of some of the most common drugs you might encounter and what they will do to you.

- **Marijuana**—also called *cannabis, reefer, pot,* or *weed.* A plant that is smoked through either a pipe, bong, or rolled cigarette. Marijuana is a depressant. Basically, it's going to make you feel lazy and silly. Not to mention that it will give you a serious case of the munchies.

- **Ecstasy**—*MDMA, EX,* or *candy.* This drug affects serotonin levels in the brain, causing euphoria and an increased awareness of sensual perception. In layman's terms, ecstasy makes you want to touch and love everything and everybody. The downside? It dangerously dehydrates the body, causes acne and premature aging, and destroys short-term memory. Not to mention that it does all kinds of damage to several internal organs. Ecstasy is rarely pure anymore, and is usually mixed with another substance such as cocaine or heroin (if you're lucky).

Worse, it might be mixed with a household cleaner such as Drano or Comet.

- **Cocaine**—or *coke*. This stuff turns you into a paranoid, hyperactive freak who thinks everything he/she does is amazing. It makes you feel like everything is the best thing you've ever seen, heard, or otherwise experienced. It is also highly addictive, expensive, and destructive. In an altered "rock" form, it can be smoked through a glass pipe and is referred to as *crack*.

- **Heroin**—Probably one of the most addictive and dangerous drugs on the market. Heroin's effects are very similar to those of ecstasy, only even more intense. Heroin addiction is one of the most difficult to break, if not the most difficult. Normally it is taken intravenously, injected with a syringe or hypodermic needle.

- **LSD**—commonly referred to as *acid*, or "*sid*" for short. This psychedelic drug can be dropped onto the tongue as a liquid or is absorbed into a small piece of square paper that can be placed under the tongue. This drug plays tricks on your head, and no one is quite sure what the long-term effects of LSD are. It is known, however, that LSD stays in the spinal column for a very long time, causing what are called "flashbacks"— short, unexpected psychedelic episodes caused by residual LSD.

It Could Happen to You _____

I was never much for the drug scene. Eventually my curiosity got the best of me. I decided to drop acid one night at a party. An hour later, nothing seemed to be happening. So I started walking home. When the drug wore off, I woke up in a tree wearing nothing but my underwear. Of course, it was just after dawn ... so I had to get back to my dorm room without being seen. Well, that didn't happen. My wallet and clothes turned up the next day ... hanging from the campus flagpole. I guess I put them up there, but I honestly don't know. Man, what a weird night.

Anonymous—School and classification withheld

GHB: The Date-Rape Drug

GHB is a new and dangerous drug that has shown up on the club scene. GHB affects memory and basic neurological functions. Across the country, young people are being victimized by sexual predators who slip this drug into their drinks and wait for it to take effect. Once the victim is under the influence of GHB, they will do just about anything because they are no longer able to resist.

Word, Yo!

GHB (Gamma Hydroxyl Butyrate)— Normally, GHB comes in the form of an odorless liquid that is salty to the taste and is sold on the street in small bottles. This drug is also sold in both powder and capsule forms. GHB is classified as a sedative-hypnotic. Originally, GHB was meant to be used as a sleep-aid. Another drug, **GBL**, is sold under as many as 80 different possible names and turns into GHB once it enters the bloodstream, causing the same effect.

The Choice of Cowards

For anyone who may be thinking about using this drug on someone else, you should know that GHB is not only unethical and immoral. It is illegal! It is known as **Drug Facilitated Sexual Assault (DFSA)** and is defined as the use of illegal narcotics to unlawfully perform sex acts upon an unwilling party.

The use of illegal narcotics by rapists has begun to gain more attention in recent years as more drugs become available to the general public. Unfortunately, this created a problem in the law. If someone was so drugged up that they did not, or could not, say "No," could it still be called a rape? Fortunately, it can. The law now provides strict criminal penalties for DFSA. Drugging their victims can no longer be used by rapists as a way to avoid prosecution.

If you choose to use GHB, you will be prosecuted if caught. Not to mention that it's a low thing to do to another human being. Learn to be social, get a girlfriend, and get a life. GHB is not the cure; it's the disease.

Word, Yo!

Drug Facilitated Sexual Assault (DFSA)—The use of illegal narcotics by rapists to render their victims unconscious and unable to resist. The law now provides strict criminal penalties for DFSA.

Campus Cautions

Remember that you should avoid having even consensual sex with someone who has either been taking drugs or is very intoxicated. This could end with you being charged with a crime you did not believe you were committing. Better safe than sorry.

How GHB Makes You Feel

In small doses (a "capful"), GHB causes you to feel a reduction in social inhibitions, similar to the effect of drinking alcohol, as well as an increase in your sex drive/libido.

In high doses, the drug induces feelings of euphoria, later giving way to feelings of sedation. Additional side effects include the following:

- Nausea, diarrhea, and vomiting
- Drowsiness
- Loss of memory similar to amnesia
- Loss of muscle control and coordination
- Respiratory problems; in higher doses, it can cause one to stop breathing
- Decrease in heart rate
- Loss of consciousness
- Sleep walking
- Decrease in body temperature

If taken in near fatal doses, GHB has been known to cause seizures and coma. And the last side effect of GHB is death.

Recognizing and Avoiding GHB

Due to widespread use of this date-rape drug, you should not accept drinks from those you do not know. Also, if you leave a drink unattended, you should not drink from it again. Go buy a new one. GHB will produce bubbles when shaken, similar to the way a soda pop reacts to being shaken. This is why GHB is so often added to carbonated beverages—it's difficult to detect.

It Could Happen to You _____

> My girlfriend had a bad experience
> with GHB. Her ex slipped GHB into her
> drink when he saw her at a bar. She had
> no idea he'd done this. He put too much
> in on purpose .... Police believe he
> planned to kill her, not rape her. Her heart
> stopped six times that night and she was
> flown to the hospital. Over a month later,
> she's still recovering, both emotionally and
> physically. The ex-boyfriend's on trial for
> the charge of attempted murder. When
> you use GHB, you know what it might do
> to the person. Slipping GHB into a per-
> son's drink is as bad as trying to kill them
> with cyanide.
>
> Dave—from Columbus, OH (School,
> last name, and classification withheld
> at his request)

GHB is commonly found in the form of an odorless, colorless liquid. However, the drug can also be
yellow, red, or blue in color. No color should ever
be ruled out. GHB is also found in white or sandy-
colored powder form. As a powder, it may be
encapsulated—though not in every case. Because
GHB is *hydroscopic* (meaning it sucks up water and
moisture), the powder can sometimes take on a
gummy consistency if the air is moist or if it comes
into contact with small amounts of water or liquid.

GHB is often sold by the "capful" on the club scene. A capful is measured using the common-sized screw caps taken off of carbonated beverages that come on plastic bottles, such as soda bottles. Due to GHB's hydroscopic nature (as mentioned previously), it can be formed into a sort of gumball and sold "by the pinch." In club terms, this is referred to as a "booger."

On the Club and Bar scene, GHB is also referred to by the following names: *GBH, liquid E, liquid X, scoop, soap, easy lay, gamma 10, "G," natural sleep-500, and gook.*

Now there's a way to fight back against date-rape drugs. At www.beveragetest.com, you can order a beverage-testing card. These GHB Cards, or Personal Test Cards, contain five reusable tests. The test reacts with a visible color change when it comes in contact with a drink that has been spiked with GHB. So if an attractive but unknown person buys you a drink, this card will come in handy in determining whether he is trying to spike your drink. I know, it sounds a little paranoid. But it's better than the alternative.

The Least You Need to Know

- Yes, you will probably encounter drinking in college. But you need to be aware of the legal issues and how much you can handle.

- Because drugs are illegal and dangerous, you should avoid them.

- The date-rape drug GHB is illegal, immoral, and potentially fatal. Avoid becoming a victim by being careful what you drink.

Dealing With Depression

In This Chapter

- Knowing the warning signs of depression
- Dealing with depression
- Recognizing suicidal behavior in yourself and others and preventing the worst from happening

We all get a little depressed sometimes, some of us more than others. Most of the time, feeling down is just a normal part of being human. However, when you are overwhelmed with sadness to the point that it is affecting your ability to function as you normally do, the problem might be a bit more serious. The truth is, college can be a big adjustment. For some students, drastic lifestyle changes are no big deal. But for others, the stress and alienation that occur in college life might be more than they can handle. Every year, the lives of many college students across the globe are brought to an abrupt and tragic end by suicide. Don't let this happen to you or someone you care about.

In this chapter, I discuss some of the common warning signs those suffering from depression exhibit. I also cover early indicators of suicidal behavior. I give you some basic methods on how to deal with these problems in yourself as well as in those around you. In summary, I am going to do all that I can to prevent the torment of depression and/or the tragedy of suicide from affecting any of your lives. Honestly, nothing is worth anyone's happiness ... and there is nothing so terrible that it is worth a single human life.

Red Flags: Recognizing Depression

Very often, an individual suffering from depression is quite unaware of the oddities in his or her own behavior. In the eyes of people suffering from depression, the behavior they are exhibiting is perfectly rational or otherwise excusable/justifiable in some way. They often do not see themselves as being depressed, necessarily. They are usually not thinking very rationally and can do little but feel hurtful, painful emotions. Depression, one might say, is that point when the mind ceases to think because one can do nothing but feel.

Someone suffering from depression, especially a close friend, is going to need all the help you can offer to get them through it. First, however, you need to know the difference between someone who is depressed and someone who is simply just down in the dumps.

It Could Happen to You

I had a roommate a few years ago who broke up with her boyfriend of three years. She stayed in bed and did nothing but cry for a week and nearly got kicked out of school. I didn't get it. She was a 4.0 student before the breakup! The saddest part is that I never once offered her my help or told anyone that she might need to see a counselor. I just left her alone and let her cope with it. I've yet to forgive myself. After a while, she did manage to recover on her own and got some help. But her once-perfect grade-point and the past trust of her professors have never recovered.

Anonymous—School and class withheld

Here are some of the telltale warning signs of a person suffering from serious depression. Remember that these signs should be seen as deviations from the individual's normal behavioral patterns. If a person has always behaved in one or more of these ways, for example, they might not be suffering from depression ... they might just be kind of weird:

- Constantly oversleeping or staying in bed throughout the day for several days to a number of weeks.

- Skipping classes for no clear or valid reason.

- Sudden and unusual lack of personal hygiene, for example, not showering, forgetting to brush teeth, refusing to put on makeup, and so on.

- Showing no interest in the things that they used to normally enjoy; for example, someone who loves to go horseback riding but declines a friend's offer to go because they "just don't feel like it."

- Constantly crying for hours or bursting into uncontrollable fits of sobbing over an unusually long period of time (as in several weeks).

- No longer looking others in the eyes when speaking to them (if they did make eye contact in the past ... some people don't).

- Shutting himself or herself off from the outside world. Exhibiting agoraphobic-like behavior, not leaving the room or another confined space for an unreasonable length of time (more than two days).

If you see any of these warning signs in yourself or in others, try first to offer an open and sympathetic ear to the person. If this fails, you might want to bring the person's behavior to the attention of an RA or some other form of mental health counselor. The longer you wait to deal with this, the harder it is going to be.

Word, Yo! _____

Depression—Lowness of spirits due to environmental influences on one's emotions and/or chemical imbalances in the brain.

Deal With It: Overcoming Depression

Although depression can be crippling, it is not impossible to overcome. Any college campus provides some form of free counseling. Crisis hotlines and support groups are available, but it is up to you to find them (whether it be for yourself or someone else). Do not ignore the warning signs until the situation leads to something much more irreversible, such as suicide or mental illness. The warning signs are given to you for a reason. When you see them, do something about it before it's too late.

Word, Yo! _____

Manic Depression or Manic-depressive Psychosis—A mental illness commonly characterized by self-degrading behavior and a melancholy disposition that alternate erratically with moments of self-assertiveness and fits of unreasonable elation or uncontrollable euphoria.

Dealing With Your Own Depression

So what do you do if you see these signs of depression and/or suicidal tendencies in your own behavior? Is it possible to protect yourself against, well ... yourself? Yes it is. Here are some methods for coping with suicidal feelings:

- Tell your therapist (if you have one already). If you don't, find a therapist, a friend, a close relative, or anyone else who might be able to speak with you and offer help.

- Avoid consuming alcohol or using any other drugs. Feelings of depression mean that you are already in an unstable mental state. You don't need to make matters worse by taking something that will hamper your rationale even further.

- Avoid doing anything that you are likely to fail at or that you find difficult until you are no longer experiencing such feelings. Know your limitations and do not attempt to surpass them until you are feeling better. Set some realistic, short-term goals for yourself and work toward each one at your own pace, one baby step at a time.

- Write out a daily schedule for yourself and stick to it no matter what happens. Decide what your priorities are and start with the things that need to be done first. Eliminate each item on your schedule as you complete it. A written schedule gives you a greater sense of stability and control over the world around you. Crossing off each task as it is completed also gives you a greater feeling of accomplishment.

- Don't forget to schedule at least two 30-minute periods for personal activities that in the past have given you some pleasure. For example, listen to your favorite music, play a musical instrument (one that you already know how to play), meditate along with doing some relaxing breathing exercises, do some needlework, read a good book or your favorite magazine, take a hot bubble bath, write a story or poem, go shopping, play a game, watch your favorite movie on DVD or video, start a garden, play with your pet (if you already have one), take a drive, or go for a walk.

- Take care of your body. Physical health and mental health often go hand in hand. Eat a well-balanced, nutritious diet instead of junk food. Do not skip any meals. Get all the sleep that you need, and go out for at least three 30-minute walks each day.

- Make sure that you spend no less than 30 minutes a day in the sunlight. Bright light is good for anyone who suffers from depression, not just those who are afflicted with Seasonal Affective Disorder (where a change in seasons can bring on bouts of depression and feelings of disorientation).

- Even though you are probably not feeling very social, make yourself speak with others.

Whether you feel like talking about your own feelings or any other topic, reduce your social isolation. This will be helpful in battling depression.

Remember that, although you might feel like the pain will never end, depression is never a permanent condition. Unfortunately, suicide (which I discuss later in this chapter) *is*.

Clinical Depression

Although serious depression is often just a stage that an individual goes through due to events or conditions in his or her environment, sometimes it's more than that. Some people are born with chemical imbalances in the brain that affect their behavior, causing extreme mood swings and depression. When this occurs, it is referred to as *clinical depression* or *manic depression*. In these cases, counseling and therapy must usually be coupled with some type of antidepressant medication.

Although these medications do come with some side effects, they are often the only way that a clinically depressed individual can cope with daily living. Taking these medications does not mean you are "insane" or a "lunatic"; it simply means that a certain neurological function in your brain is producing the wrong amounts of certain types of chemicals—hence, the reason it is called a "chemical imbalance."

It Could Happen to You

I've always been kind of moody. My family always just dismissed it. "That's just how he is," my mom would always tell people. Well, ignoring the problem only made matters worse when I eventually got out on my own and started going to college. By the end of my freshman year, I had suffered a serious nervous breakdown that resulted in my having to be hospitalized. It took another year of intense counseling and regular medication before I was ready and able to return to school. Do not ignore the problem; it will only get worse.

Anonymous—School and class withheld

The Slippery Slope to Suicide

An unfortunate result of depression and/or being overwhelmed by the stresses of life is suicide. Every year, without fail, more university students take their own lives. About 1,110 college students kill themselves each year, according to a 1997 study of suicide on Midwestern university campuses. But why, you might ask? They broke up with a boyfriend or a girlfriend. They maxed out all of their credit cards and could not afford to pay all the debt back. Their grade-point average dropped below 4.0. Any and all of these have been factors in past university-related suicides and/or suicide attempts.

Very often after a suicide or attempted suicide, everyone says they didn't even realize that the person was having any problems. They failed to notice the warning signs, the cries for help that were being offered … or they just chose to look the other way. Do not look the other way.

Suicide Signals

Here are some of the key behaviors that often indicate suicidal thoughts and tendencies:

- Asking questions such as, "If you could choose how you wanted to die, what would it be?" or "If you were going to kill yourself, how would you do it?" You should *never* answer these questions if you even remotely suspect that the person is thinking about taking his/her own life. This is an urgent warning sign—seek help *immediately*!

- Giving away sentimental and/or precious items, keepsakes such as lucky t-shirts, family heirlooms, or sentimental jewelry— anything they would not normally give away unless it was in a will. This is an urgent warning sign that this person has made up his/her mind to commit suicide. You should seek help *immediately*!

Campus Cautions

Following are three urgent warning signs that an individual has decided to take their own life. If someone you know exhibits any of these, you should seek help *immediately*!

- Asking questions about ways to die.
- Giving away treasured personal items.
- Expressing a desire or verbally wishing to die.

- Saying things that seem out of context such as, "I am going to miss you," "I wish I could just die," or "I want to die." Expressing a desire and/or verbally wishing to die are urgent warning signals of someone about to commit suicide, you need to seek help *immediately!*
- Spending more and more time alone.
- Locking their bedroom door at strange times (such as midday).
- Seeming preoccupied with the subject or idea of death and bringing up subjects related to death quite often during conversations.

It Could Happen to You

Nobody likes a tattletale. When a buddy of mine started saying, "One day, I'm just gonna kill myself," at a party. I thought he was just being drunk and stupid. I never thought he'd really do it. Well … I was wrong as #@&% about that. His parents found him in their garage the next day, in the passenger seat of his dad's truck. His head was torn apart by a 12-gauge slug. I used to say I had no regrets. Now, I have only one. I let a good friend die because I was too chicken to say, "Hey man, let's talk about this." Tell me, how stupid is that?

Anonymous—School and class withheld

Do Something About It!

Remember, suicide is not a game and it is not a joke. Do not feel like a snitch or a rat for reporting a friend's suicidal behavior to a counselor. Although you might feel guilty for doing so, that doesn't mean you shouldn't do it. I think the price of a life is worth a little guilt. Imagine how much more guilty you would feel if you did nothing while a friend or acquaintance committed suicide? Don't allow indifference to kill. Choose to intervene and help when you see someone exhibiting the warning signs of suicidal behavior.

Distance yourself from anything in your immediate environment that could be used as a means of committing suicide. For example, if you have thought about overdosing on pills, give all of your medicines (prescription as well as over-the-counter) to someone who can give them to you as you need them. Remove any dangerous objects, including any and all weapons/firearms (even kitchen knives), from your room or apartment.

It Could Happen to You

The only time I was ever truly depressed was during my freshman year. I partied myself into a big hole, maxing out credit cards for several thousand dollars. I got so overwhelmed that I locked myself in my room and didn't go to work or to class. I felt like there was no way out. My roommate tried to get me out but I refused. After 12 hours, the RA took my door off the hinges. When they found me, I had an empty bottle of pills. The doctors said if the ambulance were a few minutes later, I'd be dead ... over a few maxed-out credit cards. What a ridiculous epitaph that would have made.

Anonymous (class and school name withheld)

The Least You Need to Know

- Keep an eye out for "red flags" that indicate depression in others as well as yourself.
- Seek counseling for depression and try to find help for others who may be suffering from depression.
- Never ignore an urgent warning sign of suicidal behavior and or tendencies, never stay alone when depressed, and never leave a depressed/suicidal person alone. Seek help immediately!
- There is always hope, but those who are suffering severe depression or contemplating suicide are unable to see it. Try to show it to them.

Chapter

Stress and Managing Your Time

In This Chapter

- Recognizing the causes of stress in college
- Dealing with stress
- Mastering time management

University life can get pretty hectic, as you can probably imagine. Between classes, study groups, exams, extracurricular activities, work, and your social life, it's very easy to find yourself feeling overwhelmed. In this book, I have already discussed how to stay organized, keep your finances in order, and make time for yourself to study. All of these things will help to prevent the stressful, panic-stricken feelings of having bitten off more than you can chew from taking control of your common sense. However, being able to properly manage your time and dealing with those stresses that you simply cannot avoid are also essential to your success.

In this chapter, I talk about the common causes of stress in college life. I offer you some helpful suggestions on how to deal with stress through relaxation and other techniques, as well as how to maintain control over your busy life. You'll learn how to create a written schedule that you can follow.

Stress in College? Surely You Jest!

Stress is a major problem for anyone in a college environment. College can be a rough transition, and all the new changes to your life can make you pretty tense. Not knowing how to effectively deal with stress can make you a cranky and all-around irritable person to hang out with … and nobody wants that.

Causes of Stress

Before you can effectively find a solution to a problem, you must first be able to identify exactly what that problem is. What is it about university life that causes some students to become overwhelmed with stress and anxiety, sometimes even to the point of mental and emotional breakdown?

To better prepare you for what's to come, here are the most commonly reported causes of stress and anxiety among American university students:

- Financial strain, lack of money/funding for education/living expenses (see Chapter 3)

- Loneliness/homesickness (see Chapter 4)
- Unrealistic expectations of yourself or unfulfilled expectations
- Dating
- Expectations of parents or inability to live up to parental expectations
- Social/peer pressures
- New and/or unexpected responsibilities
- Strains on time/time urgency
- Environmental changes
- Dietary changes and/or unhealthy eating habits (see Chapter 2)
- Academic pressures (see Chapters 6 and 7)
- Learning disabilities (ADD, Dyslexia, etc.)
- Low grades
- Changes in sleeping habits and/or frequent insomnia (see Chapter 2)
- Too many extracurricular activities (see Chapter 4)
- Dissatisfaction with university life

Many of these stressors might already be familiar to you because we have discussed many of them in previous chapters. Even if you were to follow this book's suggestions to the letter, nothing can totally eliminate the presence of stress in your life (or anyone's life, for that matter). Before, during, and after college, stress will still be there.

It Could Happen to You

I was always a 4.0 student. It was a big part of my personal identity ... "who I was." I was always introduced at school functions as "Amy, a 4.0 student." When I got to college, I didn't think it would change. But I wasn't counting on catching Mono three weeks into my first semester. I caught up, and kept an "A" in all but one class. I cried my eyes out when I gave my report card to my parents—a 3.75! I thought they would never forgive me. Then my dad said, "So what? I never even got a 3.0 ... you mean more to me than a GPA."

Amy (pseudonym)—Midwestern State University

Stress is very much a part of life as a human being, not just a college student. You probably experienced a certain degree of stress in high school. And when you eventually graduate college to enter the working world, there will be new stresses to replace the ones you left behind in college. We all must suffer from stress and anxiety from time to time ... it's a part of life. The one thing that separates the relaxed people from the "stress magnets," however, is how we each deal with our own stress as individuals.

Dealing With Stress

Now that I have covered what the potential causes of stress might be, let's discuss some ways for you to deal with it. Remember, everyone is different. What works for one person might not work for another. You might already have a way of dealing with stress and anxiety. The most important thing for you to understand is that you need to deal with your anxiety, not ignore it.

Here are some suggestions to help you find your own way to becoming somewhat "stress-free" in your daily college life:

- **Meditation**—In recent years, even the scientific community has learned through experimentation that there are a number of benefits to practicing meditation techniques. Scientific studies done all over the world have indicated that regular meditation can decrease stress, anxiety, and depression, as well as lessen certain symptoms of Post-Traumatic Stress Disorder. Physiologically, meditation practitioners may even experience a decrease in Cortisol (a hormone that plays a major role in the presence of stress), stabilized blood pressure, and improvement in cardiac function. Many books and resources are available on a variety of meditative techniques.

- **Expect to have stress**—As mentioned earlier, stress is always going to be there. Why should you fool yourself? It's going to be much easier to deal with stress if you simply expect to experience it from the get-go. When you already know something is coming, it cannot catch you off your guard. So just acknowledge that college is going to be stressful and prepare for it.

- **Distract yourself**—It's always good for a person to have a hobby. Of course, not all hobbies are immediately available to us. For example, if your hobby is rock climbing, you can't just go do a quick climb to clear your head. Find something a little more immediate, such as cross-stitching, crochet, or a video game (something simple, like *Tetris*). The mental distraction does not necessarily have to be a hobby, either. Go write a poem about how you feel (but don't worry about form or rhyme), read a chapter from your favorite book, work on a puzzle, or listen to a song that relaxes you. Just do something to take your mind off the stresses in your life. Giving your mind a break will help you come back to your problems refreshed and with a more positive perspective.

- **Change something immediately**—Okay, obviously you can't just make everything "all better" with the wave of a magic wand or the twitch of your nose (if you could, you wouldn't need to go to college). What you can do, however, is to make at least one small change in the situation that is causing the stress. For example, if you are stressed out about a term paper that is due soon, go talk to a tutor in the writing lab or talk it over with your professor. Does this magically make a paper appear? No. It will, however, make the problem seem smaller and more manageable.

● **Blow off some steam**—Even if you implement all of the aforementioned tactics for battling stress, there are going to be moments when they just are not enough. The truth is, sometimes we all just need to blow off a little steam. This is best achieved, I have found, by doing an activity that is both fun and physical. Wear yourself out like there's no tomorrow. Go hit a punching bag, run yourself ragged, or dance yourself dizzy.

Keeping Control over Your Life

A main factor in avoiding unwanted and unneeded stress is to maintain control over your own workload. In college, it's very easy to bring too much upon yourself. A big part of this is learning to say "No" to people. It's great to be someone that people can rely on to get a job done. However, it's not good to let others take advantage. You are not omnipotent ... nobody is. You can't do everything and, if you are taking a full class load, too many extracurricular activities can send you spiraling right out of control.

Think of college activities in the same way you would think of a weighing scale—you have to balance out your interests with your priorities. On the one side, you will have your academic obligations; and on the other, your out-of-class activities will need to be weighed against them. The point where these two sides cease to balance each other out is whenever one of them begins to interfere with the other. Just as your extracurricular activities should not interfere with your schoolwork, you should not have so much schoolwork that you have no time for extracurricular activities or even a social life.

It Could Happen to You

My sophomore year, I bit off way more than I could chew. I became the English Club Pres., the Science Fiction Club VP, and the English Honor Society Treasurer all in the same semester. I attended two academic conferences and hosted more out-of-class events than I care to remember. The end result? I was a complete mess! I started losing sleep and my mental health began to suffer as a result. It took some hard reality checks before I realized that I couldn't do it all. The following year, I toned things down a bit and decided to put a limit on how much I would obligate myself to. It's made a significant difference in my stress level.

Nathan Brown—Junior, Midwestern State University

If you plan on being involved in a lot of student organizations, then you should not be taking a full load of classes. If, however, you absolutely *must* take a full load—in order to retain a scholarship/grant (or for any other reason), then you will need to place a well-defined limit on your level of involvement in extracurricular activities. This does not mean that you will have to drop out of any organizations to which you belong. You should, however, not accept any more than one (at the most, two) officer nominations or any other major positions of responsibility.

Managing Your Time

Now that I've discussed how to handle the stress in your life, it's time to figure out how to get all of it into some kind of coherent order. Good time-management skills are essential to helping you stay focused and on top of things.

Create a Schedule

With an up-to-date written schedule, you will always know where you need to be, and when you need to be there. Here's an example of how you might write a basic weekly schedule:

Sun	Mon	Tues	Wed	Thurs	Fri	Sat
Study Group @ 2 P.M. for History	Class 8 A.M.–12 P.M.	Class 9:30 A.M.–12:20 P.M.	Class 8 A.M.–12 P.M.	Class 9:30 A.M.–12:20 P.M.	Class 8 A.M.–12 P.M.	Sleep In
	History Exam @ 10 A.M.			Research Paper Due for English		Recover From Joey's Party
Library for Research Paper @ 6 P.M.	Club Meeting 3 P.M.		Special Lecture 7 P.M.		Party At Joey's 8 P.M.	Dancing at the Club @ 7 P.M.
			Complete Research Paper for Tomorrow			

You don't have to do your own schedule exactly as I have shown, just as long as you *do* start and keep track of one. You could, of course, always run out and buy one of those expensive little leather-bound planners. But honestly, you would do better to buy just a simple, notebook-styled, month-to-month planner. These planners are cheaper, easier to replace, and offer you a lot more space to write in than the more expensive day planners.

Survival of the Cheapest

Do not buy yourself an expensive day planner that will likely be outdated by the following year. Replacement inserts are often difficult to find for these types of corporate planners—plus, they have a lot of stuff in them that you do not need but will still wind up paying for. Your best bet is to simply buy a notebook-styled, month-to-month planner that you can get at any office-supply store for as little as a few bucks and often no more than $10.

Going Digital?

Another option you have is to shell out around $250 for one of those fancy Personal Digital Assistants (PDAs), such as a Palm Pilot. Do yourself and the rest of the university world a favor and don't buy one of these. They are expensive, complicated, and a thief magnet. Every year, I see at least one flyer posted up in the student center offering a reward for the return of some poor soul's lost PDA. The truth is, it was not *lost* … it was *stolen*.

The other problem with expensive digital planners is that, like all computers, they can malfunction (or you can make an irreversible mistake). If you forget to charge the battery and it ends up going dead, you are knee deep in something that doesn't smell very nice because you just lost all of your data. Of course, you can back up a PDA on your computer's hard drive. But who's got enough time for that?

Lastly, PDAs are easy to forget about once the initial "new toy" glamour of them has worn off. Ask anyone who has had a PDA/Palm Pilot for any extended length of time and you will often hear the same thing—"Well, it's great, but I always forget to use it." Writing stuff down is still the safest way to keep a schedule. You can't accidentally delete it, notebooks don't get viruses or malfunction, and you will never need to take a month-long class to learn how to use a pen and write stuff down.

The Least You Need to Know

- Know the causes of stress so you can deal with them as they arise. Then find a method for dealing with stress that works best for you.

- Keep a schedule of your weekly events and obligations. Buy a notebook-style planner instead of an expensive day planner, Palm Pilot, or PDA.

Index